The Clapham Train Accident

The Clapham Train Accident

Causes, Context and the Corporate Memory Challenge

Greg Morse, D.Phil FCIRO

PEN & SWORD
TRANSPORT

AN IMPRINT OF PEN & SWORD BOOKS LTD.
YORKSHIRE – PHILADELPHIA

First published in Great Britain in 2023, reprinted in 2024 by
Pen and Sword Transport
An imprint of
Pen & Sword Books Ltd.
Yorkshire - Philadelphia

ISBN 9781399073028

Typeset in INDIA by IMPEC eSolutions
Printed and bound in England by CPI Group (UK) Ltd, Croydon CR0 4YY.

Pen & Sword Books Ltd incorporates the imprints of Pen & Sword Books Archaeology,
Atlas, Aviation, Battleground, Discovery, Family History, History, Maritime, Military,
Naval, Politics, Railways, Select, Transport, True Crime, Fiction, Frontline Books,
Leo Cooper, Praetorian Press, Seaforth Publishing, Wharncliffe and White Owl.

For a complete list of Pen & Sword titles please contact

PEN & SWORD BOOKS LIMITED
47 Church Street, Barnsley, South Yorkshire, S70 2AS, England
E-mail: enquiries@pen-and-sword.co.uk
Website: www.pen-and-sword.co.uk

or

PEN AND SWORD BOOKS
1950 Lawrence Rd, Havertown, PA 19083, USA
E-mail: Uspen-and-sword@casematepublishers.com
Website: www.penandswordbooks.com

Contents

Foreword

This book is about so much more than a railway accident.

The story of the wire that was left dangling before the accident at Clapham is famous in the lore of railway safety. But this book is not about a dangling wire – it is about the real causes of the accident, many of which started years before and far away from Clapham. As Greg tells us, 'railways do not exist in a vacuum ... There's another world beyond the boundary fence, and it always plays a part.' In some cases, the impact the world is having on the railway is easy to see – but sometimes, the changes are so subtle it's not easy to foretell the unintended consequences that will arise.

Through his meticulous research, Greg takes us on a journey from the real beginnings of the story to the accident at Clapham, and in doing so creates a definitive text on railway safety.

But this book is not just an authoritative account of facts. Greg's flair for engaging storytelling highlights the most important aspect of this story: the human aspect. He describes with compassion the real lives of the people involved – from the signalling technicians who were working to provide for their families, to the managers who were trying to keep the railway running while the organisation was being restructured around them. And, most importantly, he tells us about the real lives of the victims of the accident.

The railway has learned a lot from the accident at Clapham and from other accidents that have occurred since, such as Southall, Ladbroke

Grove and Hatfield. Despite their apparent differences, this book shows us that the deeper we look, the more we see common themes in the underlying causes of these disasters.

In 1988, the world was changing rapidly; it's changing even more rapidly today. Yet some things have not changed: frontline staff are still working hard to provide for their families in the best way they can; managers are still trying to keep the railway operating despite the whirlwind of changes that are going on around them. The parallels are chillingly clear.

Nobody can predict the future, but if we improve our understanding of the past, we can better anticipate what may occur. As Greg explains, 'Yesterday is important. Yesterday is the bedrock of all that comes after.'

This book is not just about an accident that happened in 1988; it is an essential guide to understanding how the changes we make today may impact the railway we will have in the future.

Dr Peter Hughes
March 2022

Acknowledgements

S oon after joining the rail industry, I met a man who handed me a copy of *Red for Danger*. He knew he was pushing on an open door, but it ignited an interest in the history of accidents, what was done about them, and what we need to keep remembering. That man was Roger Badger, former signaller, later signalling inspector and RSSB expert on SPADs and TPWS activations. Thank you, RB.

I first started to think seriously about the Clapham accident more specifically while writing *Railway Accidents* for Shire Publications back in 2013, so my thanks go to Nick Wright, then Publisher of that company and the man who commissioned the book.

After *Railway Accidents* came an article in *Rail* magazine, looking at Clapham in greater depth. If it had not been for Nigel Harris, who invited me to write it, I would not have seen the potential for a longer treatment, so my thanks go to Nigel and the team at Bauer as well.

As to *this* book, my thanks go first to John Scott-Morgan, Janet Brookes and the crew at Pen and Sword, without whom it would not have appeared. Many grateful thanks too to Dr Peter Hughes of the University of Huddersfield, who read the manuscript twice, made excellent comments and then wrote a foreword kinder than I could have wished for.

Five friends were also kinder than I could have wished for. Marianna White (RSSB), Stuart Webster-Spriggs (VolkerRail) and Michael Woods (RSSB) all gave me more time than I'm sure they had to spare, both in reading the text and talking to me about their experiences of corporate memory loss in the rail industry right here, right now. Derek Hotchkiss generously loaned many of the source documents I was able to cite and shared his knowledge and understanding of signalling in a way that was invaluable in helping me tell the story. John Cartledge of London TravelWatch, who attended the public inquiry on behalf of the Central Transport Consultative Committee, the London Regional Passengers Committee and the Transport Users Consultative Committee for Southern England, made British Rail's internal report on Clapham available and offered unstinting advice and comment throughout the writing process.

Special thanks are due to Gordon Pettitt, who gave permission for his Septemeber 2022 interview with Kevin Martin (part of Network Rail's *Facing Points* podcast series) to be quoted.

I must also thank Terry Gourvish, official BR historian, whose generosity was greatly appreciated, and Andy Stringer, Chief Engineer at Siemens Mobility Ltd, for his insight and for demonstrating the wiring model he made to show what happened on that dark morning in 1988.

To the large number of my rail industry colleagues, friends, and officials who helped, I thank you for your thoughtfulness, insight and guidance: Dan Basacik, James Catmur, John Chalcraft (Rail Photoprints), Paul Chancellor (Colour-Rail), Matt Clements, Bridget Eickhoff, Huw Gibson, Chris Green, Andrew Hall (Chief Inspector, RAIB), Jay Heavisides, Philip Hunt, Prof Anson Jack, Heather Jager (IMF), Julia Jenkins, Clive Kessell (IRSE), David Rose, Peter Van der Mark, Paul Thomas and Steve White.

Finally, this book would also not have been possible without the excellent Railways Archive website (www.railwaysarchive.co.uk). Although a hard copy of the Hidden report was used throughout, every other railway accident report, from Polmont to Purley, Colwich to Lockington, involved this remarkable online resource. It is run by electrification engineer and noted author Garry Keenor, with Rupert Dyer and Stuart Johnson doing most of the uploading work. I recommend it to all researchers and historians.

Chapter 1

Prologue

The red beam burns against the night; the driver stops the train and waits.

Waiting. That's the lot of the train driver when the signal ahead is red: waiting in a loop for an express to pass by; waiting at a platform for the 'off'. Boring it can be, but essential it is – red means danger. It also means safe: red signals warn drivers of obstructions up ahead, points set against them, and of course other trains. So if a driver passes a signal at 'danger' – if there's a SPAD – an accident can occur.

But what if a red signal actually shows green? It *should* be impossible; it *is* very rare. Yet that's exactly what happened in 1988.

Back then – when work was well under way on the redevelopment of Liverpool Street, when the East Coast Main Line was being electrified, when there was increasing productivity, more stations, rising passenger numbers, falling subsidies – it seemed as though a golden age for rail might just be dawning.

It was around this time – amid this spirit of improvement – that resignalling schemes had also been authorised or completed at Brighton, Newcastle, York, Leeds, Leicester and Waterloo. The last was a particularly big operation, involving the replacement of ageing equipment on the busiest stretch of railway in Britain. On the evening of 27 November, a technician left a bare wire in a relay room at Clapham

Junction 'A', a huge signal box on a gantry that spanned a sea of lines at the station throat. Two weeks later, further work led it to touch a terminal, make a connection and prevent a signal from returning to 'danger' after the passage of a train.

Just after eight am on Monday, 12 December, the 6:14 from Poole was heading for the cutting where that signal stood. On board, the crowded, cowed passengers were deep in conversation, deep in their morning papers, novels, thoughts ... Green light followed green light, the usual story – except the last one should have been red. As the train rounded the curve into the cutting, its driver saw another blocking the line ahead. He applied the emergency brake, but it was too late.

The collision forced the leading coach to the right, where it struck an empty unit passing on the opposite line, killing conversations ... thoughts ... and 35 souls.

The resulting inquiries found out about the dangling wire, but found problems too with training, supervision, management and rostering. It's a basic truth about accidents: that there's always more than one cause.

Clapham was a pivotal point in British railway history. Much technology had been invented and applied to accident prevention by 1988; much more was to come. This book considers Clapham in context, charts the safety improvements that came after, charts too the checks and balances between investigators, operators and governments, and the abiding need to respect the lessons of the past, both today and tomorrow. Yet this book is also about *people*. Those named are not named to shame, but to portray the story as a human one. The concatenation of events, the errors, the reorganisations, the financial constraints, that led to Clapham could happen to any business in any industry. On the morning of 12 December 1988, they happened to the railway. Those involved were people like us, people who were trying to do their best.

A note on the text

Like many other industries, the railway has a language all its own. Common acronyms are written out in full on their first appearance. Some technical terms are <u>underlined</u>, which means that a definition may be found in the Glossary on pages 211 to 218. A number of the entries will include information more than familiar to railway enthusiasts. Safety practitioners new to rail may find them more useful.

Space prevents references to the Clapham public inquiry report from being cited as much as the author would have preferred. However, a searchable version can be downloaded from the Railways Archive website. The full wording of all the report's recommendations referred to in the book may be found on pages 219 to 221.

PART 1:

THE ELEMENTS GATHER

Chapter 2

The Journey Begins

The chapter of knowledge is very short, but the chapter of accidents is a very long one.

Lord Chesterfield, letter to Solomon Dayrolles
16 February 1753

The wire that touched the terminal in 1988 dated back to the 1930s. When new, it was part of a scheme to control signals and pointwork electrically – a cutting-edge improvement on the older mechanical means of muscle, trackside rodding, wires and pulleys. Earlier examples of this 'power signalling' existed on the London & North Western Railway at Crewe (1898), and on the South Eastern & Chatham at London Victoria (1918). Before it came to control the line through Clapham and on to Wandsworth and Earlsfield, though, there would be political change, for 1918 was also an election year.

Elections mean campaigns. In his, the leader of the post-war coalition government, Liberal MP and former chancellor David Lloyd George told of the 'fit country for heroes' that he wished to create in the grey aftermath of the Great War. It was a laudable idea that sadly came to little, but despite the ideological differences that dogged the administration elsewhere, it did manage to create a Ministry of Transport in 1919. This grouped the relevant powers of the Road Board, the Ministry of Health, and the Board of Trade into one. A similar idea, nationalisation, was also mooted at this stage, the advantages of unified command having been evident during the conflict, when the railways had been sequestrated by the government to ease the movement of troops and supplies. Winston Churchill saw the benefit of the State running them at a loss 'to develop industries and agriculture', but inflation had seen the railway wage bill rise threefold between 1913 and 1920, while a miners' strike the following year lost so much traffic that the system was thrown some £60 million into debt.

Yet the benefits of unity continued to appeal. As the first Transport Minister, Eric Geddes, put it, under a:

> 'system of competition not only did one railway ... strive to divert traffic from another, but trams sought to wrest traffic from the railways, railways to wrest traffic from canals ... and so on … In future, our effort will be to encourage each agency of transport to undertake that part of the work which it, owing to its own special qualities, can most efficiently and economically perform.'[1]

It was to be a grand scheme of integration, the intent of which was embodied in the 1921 Railways Act, which came into effect on 1 January 1923, not nationalising, but effectively amalgamating 123 smaller companies into the famous 'Big Four': the Great Western, London Midland & Scottish, London & North Eastern and Southern.

Thus the so-called post-Grouping railway was born, the one celebrated in books, featured in newsreels, films, photographs and countless recollections. The railway of the nascent media age, it still resonates with many enthusiasts, and politicians, when trying to make a point about how good the 'Good Old Days' used to be. In reality it was a difficult period for the industry, blighted as it was by improvements in road surfaces, in road vehicle technology and the post-war sell-off of hundreds of ex-military lorries, which allowed private hauliers to proliferate and undercut the railway, just as the bus and motor coach industry was doing much the same thing on the passenger side. The legislation wasn't much help either; thanks to the Rail and Canal Traffic Act of 1854 – which built on the Carriers Act of 1830 – the railways were *common* carriers, meaning they could refuse no consignment (no matter how small and unprofitable) and were obliged to publish their freight rates, thereby making undercutting all the simpler.

These issues did not, however, deter Sir Herbert Walker, the indefatigable General Manager of the new Southern Railway, of which the South Eastern & Chatham was now a part. Walker himself had come from one of the new company's other constituents, the London & South Western (LSWR), which ran services from Waterloo down to Southampton, Portsmouth, Bournemouth, Weymouth, Exeter and North Cornwall. In a bid to fight off bus and tram competition, it had started electrifying its London suburban services earlier in the century, favouring 600 volt DC carried by a third rail (current for the traction motors being collected via 'shoes' attached to the bogies of its trains). Although the Southern had inherited both this and the 6,600-volt AC overhead system adopted by the London, Brighton & South Coast Railway (LBSCR), it would be the 'third rail' that became the standard, as it was considered easier and cheaper to install and maintain than the 'overhead', whose construction was slow and whose acceleration potential was comparatively poor.

Walker truly believed in electrification. As he told a meeting of the Institute of Transport in 1921, for him it brought about 'cheaper operation, greater density of traffic, and, therefore, an increase in net revenue'. In *Sir Herbert Walker's Southern Railway* (1973), Charles F. Klapper wrote that 'we do not know positively if … Walker's ambition was for an all-electric Southern Railway, but it is highly probable that in the plans which he habitually revealed to his colleagues one short step at a time, this was the final goal'. With this in mind, those colleagues cannot have been completely surprised when, in 1929, he announced his intent to 'electrify to Brighton'. In doing so, Walker would make manifest an earlier dream; in November 1918, during the first flush of peacetime, the LBSCR had returned to the idea of electrifying a main line, so much so that its board approved a scheme that reached down to both Brighton and Eastbourne. But priorities change and in 1922 work resumed instead on electrifying the lines to Coulsdon & Smitham Downs (later Coulsdon West) and Sutton (via Selhurst). This project was still under way when the LBSCR became part of the Southern the following year. With Walker now behind the main line plan, however, two rails became three, such that Brighton was finally reached in 1933, with Eastbourne, Hastings and Seaford joining the network two years later.

Not that electrification was just about laying another rail, supplying power and replacing steam with modern unit trains. It was also about removing redundant facilities, lengthening platforms, building carriage sheds and improving track layouts. On the control and command side, four-aspect colour light signals with full interlocking were installed at many principal stations as the work progressed. This could indicate a 'red' up to two sections ahead, thus increasing traffic density and allowing more trains to be run at greater speeds. The Southern had in fact been the first to adopt four-aspect signalling, which had come into use between Holborn Viaduct and Elephant & Castle back in March 1926. The power frames at West London Junction and Clapham 'A' had been commissioned on 17 May 1936; those at Waterloo followed on 18 October.

The Way to The Sea

The new system allowed ten of the old mechanical boxes to be abolished. It also meant that our wire was now in place. For the time being, though, trains were getting faster and more frequent – benefits that, thanks to the arrival of electric traction to Portsmouth in July 1937, were also being enjoyed on the old LSWR's old South Western Main Line … though only as far as Woking, where the Portsmouth line diverged. Beyond Woking, on the other side of the junction, steam still reigned supreme.

Imagine taking an express to the west around this time. Arriving at what O.S. Nock called 'one of the really great stations of the world', you'd find yourself no longer lost in the 'rambling rabbit warren of nooks, crannies, additions, extensions, arches, alleys and confused humanity which made up the old Waterloo,'[2] nor as confused as Jerome K. Jerome's *Three Men in a Boat* when they sought a train to Kingston, failed to find anyone who knew about it and finally slipped the driver of an Exeter service half a crown to take them there. No, now you would find 'twenty-one platforms ranged in a crescent facing west', the station having been extended in 1885 and rebuilt between 1901 and 1922.[3] Not having anyone to meet under the famous clock over the concourse, you'd show your ticket at the gate and walk along the platform to board a compartmented carriage of the Maunsell era, at the head of which was standing perhaps a high-stepping Drummond T9. The guard's whistle would blow, the driver would open the regulator, and the journey would begin, the train puffing its way over endless brick arches, over – as *Bradshaw* had described it – 'the tops of houses, past the grounds of Lambeth Palace'. If you looked across the river, you might see the Houses of Parliament, before you passed through Clapham Junction, through a cutting opposite Spencer Park and – as John Betjeman would describe it – on towards 'the coniferous half-world of Woking' and 'the slippery heather and rhododendrons of Aldershot'.

More powerful engines still would come after Oliver Bulleid took over as the Southern's Chief Mechanical Engineer in 1937, his

'Merchant Navy' 'Pacifics' soon powering boat trains, *Belles* and the *Atlantic Coast Express* westwards, often with elegant Pullman carriages in tow, where breakfast, morning coffee (and sometimes something stronger) could be enjoyed on the move. For the commuter, though, it was somewhat different, crowded – as commuters often were, often are – in their swift electrics. Tired, disgruntled Pooters heading not to Holloway but to a street in, say, Battersea, might see naught but the person standing, swaying next to them, as they tried to turn the pages of the *Illustrated London News, Daily Sketch* or *Sporting Life*. They might smell that musty, fusty end-of-day smell that clings to the body as shadows lengthen and evening comes. They might yelp as a hobnail boot accidentally crunched their toes. The best thing about commuting is not commuting, so alighting at Clapham Junction would bring joy, if not eternal, then enough at least to propel them to their own street, their own front door and the comparative sanctuary behind it.

Summer of '67

Fast forward to the early 1960s and commuting might not have changed much, but the Southern Railway had become the Southern Region of the nationalised British Railways (BR). At the end of 1954, BR had published a plan to modernise. It was a bid to curb its losses, as motor car ownership went up, operating costs went up, fares lagged, even more freight was lost to the roads and recruitment grew harder, as fewer men wanted to get covered in soot and grime cleaning, firing and maintaining locomotives (despite what some of them might have thought as boys). For the Southern – and the South Western Main Line – it would mean electric traction for commuters and long-distance travellers alike, as steam began to breathe its last. While the third rail was being laid from Woking to Bournemouth, therefore, and while most trains remained in the charge of Bulleid's mighty snorting steeds, many drivers enjoyed a last hurrah.

The magic 'ton' was reached on several occasions, but when No. 35003 *Royal Mail* touched 106mph between Winchfield and Fleet as it worked from Weymouth on 26 June 1967, it was the last time a steam-hauled service train did so in Britain. All too soon the end came and went, leaving the new order to take over from Monday 10 July.

On the one hand, electrification brought sleeker services and higher passenger numbers; on the other, it condemned Southern spotters to a diet of bland multiple units, which did little to stir the blood. They weren't exactly state-of-the-art, either: the electrification package had been accepted on the understanding that existing rolling stock would be reused. The twenty-eight four-car and three three-car unpowered units were therefore converted from Mark I carriages, which had been designed the decade before, traction being supplied by new (but similar) '4-REP' electric multiple units, built at York works.

The start of the new service was not without problems, diesel haulage being required on some trains, thanks to teething problems with the new electrics. As *Railway World* reported in its September issue, staff unfamiliarity with the workings – which allowed little margin for delay in attaching and detaching the branch portions of through trains, for example – also contributed to 'probably the worst weeks of chaos that the Southern has ever known'. Yet for British Transport Films (BTF), for British Rail too, the death of steam on the Bournemouth line had made travel 'clean, quiet, fast and frequent' – 'fit for the '70s', in fact. No longer would there be 'muck everywhere'. No longer would it get 'in your eyes, your ears, in your hair'. No longer would smoke obscure the lushness of the New Forest or the majesty of Winchester. Now, longer-distance commuters like the young gent in 1967's *Speedrail to the South* would be able to enjoy a breath of sea air at his Bournemouth home, a fine fried breakfast on board and a trouble-free passage to his London office, all inside 100 minutes. Southern Regional Manager David McKenna told the local newspaper that 'an improvement in passenger revenue of £1.1 million' was expected over the next ten years.

Everyone would be a winner – even those who lived in Weymouth, for though there were insufficient funds for electrifying beyond Bournemouth, BR adopted a combination of push-pull operation and an ingenious method of working, whereby non-powered carriages were 'pushed' from the capital by a 4-REP being driven from a cab in the non-powered end of the train. On arrival at the Dorset resort, the REP would be uncoupled and an adapted diesel-electric would hook on and haul the carriages the rest of the way. The diesel would then 'push' them back to Bournemouth, where the waiting 'tractor unit' would take over for the return to London.

On the whole, the system settled down and worked well – so much so that the push-pull part of the operation would soon be adopted at the opposite end of the country. Not that old Mark I stock would be used there, but something much more sturdy. Which was just as well, as it turned out.

Chapter 3

A Good Idea

It was beautiful and simple as all truly great swindles are.
O. Henry, *Gentle Grafter*, 1908

Anyone travelling between Edinburgh and Glasgow in 1961 would have found steam supplanted by a Swindon-built <u>diesel multiple unit</u>. Dating from 1956, put into service the following year, they were faster and more comfortable than what had gone before. As a result, they boosted traffic by some 7 per cent a year, and also helped cut pollution in and around Waverley station (about which the Edinburgh Corporation had expressed concern).

By 1966, a timetable change was providing a fast train each way every hour, but within two years passenger numbers were falling back, as the 8.8 million cars on British roads in 1967 grew towards 9.6 million by 1969. Worse was arguably to come, the construction of the M8 – which would link Scotland's two major cities – being well under way at this point. An upgrade was clearly needed. Thankfully, that call was about to be answered.

In 1968, the Scottish Region set up a planning committee to help bring the line into line with similar routes elsewhere on the network. Recognising that the Southern had had a good idea, that year's National Traction Plan made reference to 'Type 4 locomotives for push-pull working between Edinburgh and Glasgow'.[4] 'Type 4' meant power, specifically something in the region of 2,500hp. And while trials had been conducted with a lower-rated, specially adapted <u>English Electric Type 3</u> that February, by April similar tests were being held with one of the same manufacturer's latest Type 4s – the Class 50, fifty of which had been delivered between October 1967 and December 1968 to help speed up services on the non-electrified northern section of the West Coast Main Line.

These new blue beasts were rated for 100mph running, but though they had been fitted with the circuitry for push-pull operation from new, interference from some of the other wiring on board meant that it did not work well. And while the locomotive selected for the trials – D405 – certainly attained the 'ton', it suffered five engine shutdowns in the process, requiring the fitter to make impromptu repairs 'on the hoof'. These problems could doubtless have been overcome, but other events would soon conspire to force a change.

The Quest for Speed

Market research had found that, for journey times of up to three hours, rail was the mode of choice and had the added advantage of delivering travellers close to shops and office blocks. Beyond three hours, people tended to decamp to the domestic airlines. When the £55 million project to electrify from Weaver Junction right through to Glasgow was approved in February 1970, BR sought to make an interim improvement by rostering pairs of 50s for the section beyond Crewe, which included the punishing gradients of Shap (1 in 75) and Beattock (1 in 67).

A Brush-built Type 4 ('Class 47') had also been tested on the push-pull runs, but with the prospect of *no* 50s available for the Edinburgh–Glasgow shuttle, the Scottish Region looked instead to another airline-combating project being considered by BR's engineers – the high-speed diesel train (HSDT). A good idea is a good idea, and the basic one behind the HSDT was a set of newly designed carriages bookended by power cars equipped with 2,250-hp Paxman Valenta engines. The latter revved at around twice the rate of their contemporaries and were light enough to increase route availability and avoid track damage. The aim was 125mph operation.

The Scottish Region did not have power cars with 2,250hp engines, but – by 1970 – it did have all sixty-nine 1,250hp Class 27s, which – like their Southern brethren – had also been built by the Birmingham Carriage & Wagon Works. The idea was to create what author Colin Marsden later called a 'poor man's' High Speed Train (HST). A number of Class 27s duly had the requisite control equipment fitted, twelve retaining their steam heating boilers, twelve having them replaced by a small diesel engine and generator to provide an electric train supply. Tests took place in March 1971, with a half-hourly service starting from 3 May. The new technology, the new(ish) Mark II coaches, and new track (realigned at certain points) meant that the 47-minute journey to Glasgow could now be made in 43 minutes, meant too that Scotland had one of the best Inter-City services in Britain.

So it did, and despite occasional reports of locomotive failures and substitutions, at first it was very successful, traffic growing well until 1975. Soon, though, motor vehicle competition would flex its muscles yet again; soon the intensity of the operation would impact on the locomotives even more; soon passengers would find one or more of the pairings replaced by other classes. By June 1975, indeed, *The Railway Magazine* was lamenting that the service 'continue[d] to suffer mishaps and breakdowns' and was 'not yet provid[ing] the standard … one would expect'.

On the infrastructure side, costs were high, as the increase in traffic density increased track wear, and therefore the track maintenance requirement. On the traction side, costs were high and availability demonstrably low. The need for Type 4 power was evident, but when the West Coast Main Line electrification project was completed in 1974, the 50s were used to replace older, non-standard locomotives on services out of Paddington. From October 1976, the production HSTs began to work out of the same terminus, and this allowed the Western to release some of its Class 47s. By the middle of 1977, a plan had been formed to use them 'Southern style' between Edinburgh and Glasgow. A good idea is a good idea, after all. Both Board and Department of Transport agreed, approving the scheme later that year.

Although lower-powered than a 50, it was understood that a single Class 47 would cut costs, be kinder to the track and (coupled with a further track and signalling upgrade) raise maximum speeds from 90mph to 95. Two-wire Time Division Multiplex (TDM) technology would allow a converted locomotive to be controlled from its own cab or a 'driving brake second open' (DBSO) at the other end of the train. Twelve Class 47s were duly fitted with TDM equipment and long-range fuel tanks, becoming 47/7s in the process. Their trains largely comprised the comparatively luxurious air-conditioned 'HST' (Mark III) coaches, which offered a step-change in quality to passengers, allowing them too to step from a cold platform into an elegant bright yellow vestibule, to marvel at the saloon door that swished open like the Starship *Enterprise* and settle back in a blue tartan Second Class seat that was (hopefully) in line with a window.

Services began in October 1979 and were followed by the film cameras a few months later. The result was *Partners in Prosperity*, which focused on what seemed to be a positive era of enhancement, modernisation, and co-operation, the narrative pointing to plans for improved integration between road and rail transport north of the border. This was 'a common sense answer', and British Rail's side of it covered new station buildings at Barrhead and Larbert, new signal boxes, a new Travel Centre at Aberdeen, improved Trans-Clyde services and new freight flows. The outlook for Inter-City seemed especially bright, what with the HSTs bringing Scotland closer to the rest of Britain via the East Coast Main Line, and the Advanced Passenger Train (APT) set to do the same via the West. The new push-pull services were already doing it for Edinburgh and Glasgow, of course, using trains that were fast, efficient, and perfectly safe.

Or so it seemed.

Chapter 4

The Crumbling Edge?

How seldom is it that theories stand the wear and tear of practice!
Anthony Trollope, *Thackeray*, 1879

W hen Orwell's *Nineteen Eighty-Four* appeared in 1949, its vision of a grey, post-nuclear world of lies made many fear for the future. In some ways they would be right, but away from the world of politics, the real-life 1984 presented a world where change had come more slowly – new Mini Metros zipped past old Morris Minors, teenagers zipped up skinny jeans while Mum donned her flares and Madonna hit the Top Ten while albums by John Lennon and King Crimson hit the racks at Our Price.

It was the same on the railway, where new Class 58s hauled freights alongside twenty-five-year-old 25s, and the HST network spread as ageing 501s went on working out of Broad Street (for a little while longer at least). Practices and procedures also reflected this mixture of old and new, the latter taking time to replace the former – sometimes never quite doing so. Soon after becoming BR Board chairman in 1976, Peter Parker had warned of the need to address what he saw as BR's 'crumbling edge of quality'.[5] He'd gone by 1984, but the juxtaposition of the replaced with what needed replacing lingered on. Signalling was a prime example, with its mix of nineteenth-century semaphores, 1930s colour light signals, 1960s multi-aspects and 1980s Radio Electronic Token Block (RETB) equipment. The last was of course the latest, being a communication system that linked cab to signal cabin and did away with the need for lineside equipment like cables, telegraph poles and the signals themselves. Trialled between Dingwall and Kyle of Lochalsh in 1984, the equipment would soon come to the Wick/ Thurso, Fort William, Mallaig and Oban lines, allowing several staffed signal boxes to be closed.

Elsewhere on the Scottish Region, progress continued insomuch as the new push-pull services had proved so successful that their reach had been extended to Aberdeen. Many more passengers were able to bask in HST comfort at something closer to HST speed. Many more would praise the services, and BR for providing it. Then came an accident that called the whole operation into question.

Cow on the Line

Shortly after 17:45 on 30 July 1984, the 17:15 Glasgow–Edinburgh slowed to 30mph, thanks to restrictive aspects just beyond Falkirk. Routine stuff – frustrating, maybe – but routine … until, that is, the driver caught sight of a cow from the corner of his eye. The beast had got itself up the bank and was doing what cows do best – chew grass.[6]

When the train pulled in to Polmont a couple of minutes later, the driver told his assistant to inform the station staff. As the assistant crossed the platform, the 17:30 Edinburgh–Glasgow powered by on the Down. If the cow had actually been on the track, or if there had been a whole herd on the bank, the driver would have stopped sooner, put down <u>detonators</u>, used <u>track circuit clips</u>, phoned the signaller. *But it was all right, there was no real danger …*

The 17:30 had already reached 85mph as it passed Polmont Signal Box and took the gentle curve into the cutting beyond. The guard had finished checking tickets and returned to his compartment. The driver, controlling the train from the DBSO, suddenly saw the cow on the line and rammed on the brakes. Though he reacted quickly, it was too late to prevent a collision. The DBSO struck the animal and dragged its carcass along before the leading left-hand wheel flange lifted and rode the top of the rail. When the right-hand wheel lost purchase, the coach clattered along the sleepers before it struck the <u>cess</u> rail and veered up the bank.

Forward momentum caused the DBSO to slide, twist and collide with the third coach, which had run past it. The second coach was pushed up the opposite side of the cutting, where it divided from the train and turned end-for-end. It was now, at about 17:55, that another train slowed for a 'double yellow'. What the driver saw before him he could scarcely believe – a cloud of dust and what he would later describe as a coach 'somersaulting into the air'. His emergency brake application certainly stopped a secondary collision, certainly saved lives … but 13 people had already been killed. Seventeen more suffered serious injuries – including the driver of the 17:30, John Tennent of Eastfield Depot, who was taken unconscious to the Falkirk Royal Infirmary with a fractured skull. This time it wasn't BTF recording the scene when the cameras came, but the BBC. The lens focussed first on the locomotive – 47707 *Holyrood* – before falling on the wreckage. The reporter told of 'Britain's worst rail disaster for seventeen years', a reference to the Hither Green accident of 1967, in which 49 people had died. Vivian Chadwick, BR's Regional Operations Manager, Scotland, told of the animal remains. Survivor Herbert Robinson told of the 'carnage' and how he'd helped others escape to the lineside. He later told *The Times* that there'd been a palpable absence of panic among all involved.

BR launched an internal investigation, but the accident was also investigated by the Railway Inspectorate (RI). The Railway Regulation Act 1840 had (*inter alia*) created the RI to 'provide for the due

Supervision of Railways' for 'the Safety of the Public'. Initially, its inspectors could 'enter upon and examine' railway works, buildings and rolling stock, but had no actual authority to investigate accidents. This, it was felt, kept the responsibility for managing railways with the railways themselves. Nevertheless, the RI did conduct inquiries and submit reports to parliament in the hope that companies might be 'persuaded' to adopt safer working methods, better equipment and so on; persuaded, that is, until the Regulation of Railways Act 1871 granted it official powers to investigate accidents and report their findings formally to the Board of Trade.

The RI's first inspectors had been recruited from the Corps of Royal Engineers, most civil engineers already being in the railways' employ. This tradition was still in place in 1984, thus it was Major A.G.B. King who looked into Polmont and presented his findings the following February.

King concluded that there was a chance element in the derailment itself, as a specific part of the cow had to have been struck at a specific moment, on a specific trajectory, to lift the wheel with sufficient force to derail the train. But as the cow had accessed the line through a vandalised fence at an abandoned level crossing, he recommended a review of the way fences were inspected, and the way damage was reported, adding that 'where push–pull operation is to be introduced, improvements to fencing must be considered as part of the route development'. He also recommended that the railway's Rule Book be changed to make sure large animals within the boundary fence were treated 'as an immediate danger to trains', and that driver-to-shore communication be fitted in the cabs of all trains travelling at 100mph and over. As a result, BR changed its rules and invested some £3 million in the National Radio Network (NRN), which was introduced from 1986. Focus then fell on the DBSO.

King noted that the axleload of a DBSO was just 8.4 tonnes but added that BR had not seen a need to increase it, as it was similar to both its own multiple unit fleet and to push-pull trailers in use on the Continent. King considered the feasibility of increasing the DBSO axleload but found that 'the most that [could] be achieved without building a completely new vehicle [was] an increase to 12 tonnes, which in any case [would] take time and involve considerable modification and expense'. However, he believed the fitting of an obstacle deflector would 'provide protection commensurate with the maximum speeds involved'. His recommendation to fit such a device to the DBSO fleet was put in hand. For speeds in excess of 100mph – as was intended for Anglo-Scottish services, perhaps pushing the Sixties Southern idea to its limit – King recognised that the consequences of a collision became progressively greater but noted that a separate study into the subject was already under way.

Flashing Yellow Aspects

Although the railway learned from Polmont, plucking the flower of safety from the nettle of danger, the need to do so would soon come again. At Morpeth the month before, a southbound 'sleeper' had been derailed on a curve with a radius of just 285 metres, narrowly missing two houses. Sharp curves mean lower speeds – in this case 40mph. The train had been travelling at more than double that. The train jack-knifed, partly overturned and hit two bungalows. No one was killed, but twenty-nine passengers and six crew members were taken to hospital. Among them was the driver, who suffered a bad cut over his eye, a broken collar bone and a badly lacerated leg. He would later remember nothing of the accident, but did remember downing a scotch, a pint and a couple of cans of lager before taking charge of the train. He also thought he'd 'had a coughing fit, hit his head and knocked himself unconscious' immediately prior to the accident. A jury later agreed – he did have a long history of bronchitis, after all. In his report, Lieutenant-Colonel Townsend-Rose felt it more likely that the driver had fallen 'fully or nearly asleep'. Either way, his actions had led directly to the accident. Driver action (or inaction) would also be behind the fatal accident at Colwich Junction in Staffordshire on 19 September 1986, although the truth about Colwich was more complicated than that.

Just after 18:20 that day, Signaller Millward at Colwich box realised the 17:00 Euston–Manchester Piccadilly was approaching Colwich Junction at about the same time as the 17:20 from Liverpool.[7] As the former was running late, he decided to allow the latter through, so it could continue to run at line speed. The 'Manchester' would be crossing the path of the 'Liverpool', so he signalled it to cross first from the Down Fast line to the Down Slow. This meant its driver was shown a flashing 'double yellow' and a flashing 'single yellow', caution signals recently introduced to give fast trains advance warning of a divergent route. The train passed them and came upon a steady single 'yellow', meaning that the next signal would be red. And so it was. But the driver had expected it to clear. It did not. It remained red to protect the 'Liverpool'. The driver applied the emergency brake … too late. As the 'Manchester' approached the flat ('diamond') crossing, the driver and the trainee riding with him realised a collision was inevitable. They jumped from the locomotive just before the 'Liverpool' struck it. They and all the passengers of both trains survived. They'd been lucky. Eric Goode, the Crewe-based driver of the 'Liverpool', had not. Neither had the nine people killed when a train struck a van at Lockington level crossing on 26 July 1986, nor the driver and three passengers drowned on 19 October 1987, when a Swansea–Shrewsbury service fell into the River Towy, Glanrhyd Bridge having been partially washed away by swollen waters. A local farmer had seen that a central section of the bridge was missing. He tried to get home to telephone a warning, but hadn't been able to make it in time …

A collision, an overspeed derailment, a SPAD, a crossing accident, a bridge collapse: there seemed to be no theme, nothing to suggest an emerging trend. Was the crumbling edge of quality crumbling away? Or was it just misfortune?

Chapter 5

Sectorisation, Strikes…and Serpell

All that glisters is not gold…

William Shakespeare, *The Merchant of Venice*

I
t may not have been the best of times, but it certainly wasn't the worst – far from it, in fact. Despite Polmont, despite Morpeth, Colwich, Glanrhyd and Lockington, safety on the railways was improving. In the decade so far, three years – 1980, 1982 and 1985 – had seen no passengers killed in train accidents, a quite remarkable achievement at the time. As rail safety officer and historian Stanley Hall was to write, 'In the 10 years 1976-1985, 45 passengers lost their lives in train accidents on BR, which is about as many as are killed on Britain's roads in two or three *days*, and fewer than died in one single airline disaster at Manchester Airport [1985, 55 dead].' There was a sense that accidents on the scale of Harrow & Wealdstone (1952, 112 dead) were in the past. And, besides, the main problem of the present seemed to be not safety, but security – *financial* security.

Since its inception – as the Railway Executive – in 1948, BR had (by definition) been under the financial control of the government. Thus, when it sat below the British Transport Commission, the latter was headed by a professional civil servant, who often angered professional railwaymen by querying what were to them clear and obvious decisions. Yet this and the march for modernisation that began in the Fifties aside, it would be the Sixties that saw the most seismic shifts, when – (in) famously – Dr Richard Beeching was brought in from ICI to head a new, streamlined British Railways Board and tasked by Minister of Transport Ernest Marples to 'make the railways pay'. Beeching's report, *The Reshaping of British Railways* (1963), heralded a greater focus on the block movement of freight and the introduction of more modern management techniques. It also recommended the closure of many loss-making lines and stations, a scheme that would have seen the railway's total route mileage cut from 20,000 to 8,000, all with the aim of putting BR in the black by 1970. As it turned out, these policies would only contain the deficit, and by the Eighties the pressure to cut costs was mounting once again.

The trouble was that while the new push-pull trains were doing good business in Scotland, BR's now-ageing commuter fleet was growing more unreliable, the upturn in business fostered by the Western's HSTs was being threatened by the M4 and M5 motorways, and the <u>sparks effect</u> of the London Midland's West Coast Main Line electrification was suffering from fares increases and the launch of highly competitive Anglo-Scottish flights by British Airways.

The idea of <u>sectorisation</u> – dividing the company into distinct business units – had been hinted at after the 1979 General Election, which had seen Labour ousted by the Conservatives following a series of strikes over a public sector pay freeze imposed to control inflation. There was a realisation that there would be little chance of Margaret Thatcher's new regime investing in rail unless something was done to increase productivity. With this in mind, *Challenge of the '80s,* published that November, outlined the Board's aim to develop its commercial strengths. That same month, the government announced a subsidy reduction of £9million for 1980/81; targets for InterCity services, freight and parcels traffic were also agreed, the intent being that these would become 'self-supporting'.

The reasons behind these aims will be considered in Chapter 7, but to help achieve them, in January 1982 BR did sectorise, by splitting its operational division into five: Inter-City, London & South East, Provincial, Railfreight, and Parcels. In time, this would put BR on more of a business footing than even Beeching had envisaged. In time, each sector would develop its own identity, but the main idea was to allow their directors to keep a close eye on running costs and overheads, with a view to cutting subsidy, creating confidence and building the case for investment. It sounded like the perfect solution to BR's problems, although some managers remembered the wise words cited by celebrated railway manager Gerry Fiennes (1906–1985) that 'when you reorganise, you bleed', and feared that fragmentation would erode the clear chains of command and communication essential to safety.[8] It also was not quite enough for the government, which wanted more cuts. BR was not really in a position to argue, having been embroiled in a bitter dispute with drivers and guards over flexible rostering and the single manning of trains. There'd been threats to close the railway, threats to sack the strikers, but in the end an agreement was reached after pressure from the Trades Union Congress.

Agreement? Well yes, but the truth was that no one came out of it very well; drivers found themselves portrayed as backward-looking and unpatriotic, Parker's reputation for good labour relations was shattered and the unions failed to block flexible rostering. Yet perhaps the most severely hit had been the business itself, the dispute costing BR at least £60 million. As passenger miles fell from 18,500 million in 1981 to 16,900 million in 1982, and freight tonnages carried dropped from 154.2 million to 141.9 million in the same twelve-month period, this was a loss it could have done well without. The Board tried to ease the situation by reducing fares and the number of services, but it was clear that more money was needed.

There were two strands to think about, the core business of running trains, and the subsidiaries like ferry organisation Sealink and catering arm Travellers-Fare. BR had reorganised the latter as separate functions and hoped to sell shares to raise funds to help them flourish. At first, the government seemed amenable to the suggestion, but had changed its mind by October 1981, believing a sell-off to be the most effective way of reducing BR's drain on the public purse (as it was inevitably seen and described). British Transport Hotels was the first to go, in 1983; the rest would follow within six years. Whitehall, though, remained equally 'short-termist' where investment in the core was concerned, its approval for East Anglian electrification in December 1981, for example, being soon cut back by the rejection of the Cambridge-Bishop's Stortford and Royston-Shepreth Junction sections (thereby turning a £41 million scheme into a £30 million one).

A question mark also floated above the East Coast Main Line, which had been a key part of the Board's *Review of Main Line Electrification* (1981), undertaken with the Department of Transport. Electrification, said the report, would reduce the railway's dependence on oil and 'assist the UK manufacturing industry to win more orders overseas, in an expanding market'. It would also 'show an internal real rate of return of about 11 per cent', if the larger schemes were completed. Before the findings could be presented to the cabinet, however, the right-wing Central Policy Review Staff stepped in. More specifically, Thatcher wanted her personal economic adviser Alan Walters – former Cassel Professor of Economics at the London School of Economics – to evaluate it. Walters was no friend of nationalised industries and was known to favour a smaller railway network. As might have been expected, his scrutiny served to weaken BR's case, and helped align ministerial attitudes to electrification with the commercial viability (or not) of Railfreight and InterCity.

A dark problem, but Parker could see a glimmer of light in the form of an independent review that had come out of his discussions with the Department. It was being led by BR Board member Sir David Serpell, who left to take on the role and was regarded by both sides as a safe pair of hands. Unfortunately, his committee's report – *Review of Railway Finances*, published in January 1983 – belied his reputation and seemed to lack focus. The document was critical of BR management, aspects of its ticketing policy and engineering costs, concluding that line closures would be needed if subsidies were to be 'lowered substantially'. To illustrate the point, the committee presented six network options, from a 'high-investment' version consisting of the existing 10,370 route miles (less a planned reduction of 300) to the 'Beeching-like' Option A, which assumed a network size of just 1,630 miles.

The Board had little choice but to shunt Serpell into a siding, which it did by nudging the media towards Option A and the threat of commuter fare increases. While accepting that improvements could be made in engineering and government interaction, BR also formally condemned the report, pointing out that the mathematical model on which its network models were founded were 'inadequate to form a basis for public policy decisions', that the 'projected [cost] savings [took] no account of increased costs elsewhere in the system or of possible losses in revenue' and that the whole thing paid 'too little attention … to the expectations of customers'. Shelved pending the June 1983 General Election, it quickly lost all credibility. Parker would later write that Serpell had at least 'cleared the air'. In time, it would also give BR the impetus to pursue efficiency and 'firm up' its investment management practices. By then, though, the railway would have a new chairman.

Parker had agreed to a two-year extension of his contract in September 1981 to work on the productivity question and steer the government towards a longer-term plan. Yet he knew the next phase of BR's development had to be led from within and Robert Reid, who had joined the London & North Eastern Railway as an apprentice in 1947, was the ideal candidate. The government had wanted another 'outsider', favouring the then head of Thorn EMI, Sir Richard Cave. But Cave wanted to be a part-time deputy and Parker wanted Reid. In some ways the two were very different: Parker, the great motivator, was happy to fight Whitehall on policy and funding; Reid, the brusque, task-oriented manager, was keen to get the job done within government guidelines. Yet both had seen sectorisation as the way forward.

In the event, Parker got his wish, Reid taking over the helm in September 1983. For some, the railway was about to enter a new golden age.

Some, but not all.

Age of the Train?

Reid recognised that 'the way to prosper in any business is to satisfy the customer by giving value for money'. He went on to preside at a time when BR began to flourish, as new liveries replaced the old, receipts started to rise and relics of the steam age vanished with gathering speed. And though the company's new marketing slogan – 'We're getting there' – would be a poor heir to the previous 'This is the Age of the Train', it came to encapsulate the second half of the 1980s with some accuracy. Not all sectors would fare equally, of course.

Provincial, for example, tended to inherit everyone else's 'cast-offs'. This was particularly the case on the Cardiff–Portsmouth and Manchester Victoria–Leeds routes, where older locomotives and former main-line rolling stock soldiered on. In fact, this process – 'cascading' – was an economical way to redeploy carriages and locomotives when funds for new equipment were in short supply. The quest for cost-effective efficiency was evident too on London & South East (LSE). Here, Sector Director David Kirby had managed to cut his subsidy requirement by just over a third, reacting to a reduction in demand by withdrawing redundant stock and running fewer, shorter, trains. With much of LSE's revenue coming from commuters, though, his only hope for a large revenue increase was a new non-stop service linking London Victoria with Gatwick, devised at Board level to tap into a rise in air travel. Again, the trains made good use of older, air-conditioned, carriages and Class 73 electro-diesels, while (again) push-pull working (with a powered 'motor luggage van') afforded a quick turnaround and an intense 15-minute timetable. Launched in May 1984, the 'Gatwick Express' was so successful (one could argue) that it was shunted to InterCity the following year, doing wonders no doubt for that sector's profit margin.

While unfortunate, the transfer did not seem to deter Chris Green, who took over from Kirby in January 1986. There had been an attempt under the latter to try to enhance LSE's image by introducing new tri-tone liveries for inner-suburban, outer-suburban and express units, but the arrival of Green brought more radical change. Green had joined BR as a management trainee in 1965. As General Manager of the Scottish Region, he'd used surplus funds to erect new fencing along many routes in the wake of Polmont and had been instrumental in creating a new 'ScotRail' brand for services north of the border. Under him, London & South East was given a catchier title – Network SouthEast (NSE) – and a striking white, red and blue colour scheme. It was also expanded to bring together all commuter routes into the capital. To advertise – and galvanise – NSE, Green modernised his 930 stations, which meant branding anything and everything and saw bright red litter bins, lamp-posts and clocks spring up on platforms from Weymouth to Banbury, Bedwyn, Brighton, King's Lynn, Clacton, Clapham and Shoeburyness. He also started an initiative which allowed passengers to travel anywhere on NSE for just £3; on the first of these 'Network Days' – 21 June 1986 – 200,000 people took up the offer, most (as Green would later recall) seemingly bent on getting to the Isle of Wight![9]

As inheritor of the Advanced Passenger Train, InterCity had a slightly different problem. After a disastrous attempt to run a public service,

the train had become something of a national joke. This was not only
disheartening, it was also bad for business. In a bid to move the project
forward, the Board brought in a team of consultants, who concluded
that the technology was generally sound, but that the management team
had lacked leadership and vision (although this charge could also have
been levelled at the government, whose vacillations had hardly helped).
BR duly appointed a dedicated project manager and soon 'got a grip'
– so much so that, by 1983, the trains were beginning to work well and
by December 1984 had set a new record of 3 hours 52 minutes for the
Euston to Glasgow run. Sadly, it was a victory too late, for the fact was
that even these timings were no longer enough to tempt Anglo–Scottish
travellers away from air travel. Despite this, InterCity knew that by
raising the maximum speed of certain key expresses from 100mph to
110mph, and by adding more station stops, it could capture the key
markets of Manchester, the West Midlands and Lancashire, which were
all within the critical three-hour threshold from London within which
the train could match the plane.

When the APT was finally abandoned in 1986, InterCity also
looked again at the quality of service; on-board catering improved,
'Second Class' became 'Standard Class' and named trains were
reborn, meaning that passengers could catch the 'Cornish Riviera' to
Cornwall or the 'Master Cutler' to Sheffield just as in the glory days
of steam. It was fortunate for Reid, for BR, its passengers and freight
customers, that he got on so well with Nicholas Ridley, Margaret
Thatcher's Secretary of State for Transport from 1983. As Reid's
biographer George Muir wrote, they were similar men: both had been
cut from the same cloth, both enjoyed fishing and both 'understood
and trusted each other'. This empathy, and the fact that Thatcher
trusted Ridley, led to investment and a corporate plan backed on the
basis that a reduction in the government's financial support could

be brought forward. This is how electrification came to Cambridge, Norwich and Weymouth, though it was the East Coast Main Line that needed it most; since the demise of the powerful Deltic locomotives in 1982, the route had been in the hands of eight-car HSTs; when passenger numbers rose later in the decade, many found themselves forced to stand in the carriage aisles and vestibules, setting off the internal sliding doors to no-one's advantage.

Government approval for electrifying this premium line finally came in July 1984 and brought the prospect of more powerful locomotives that could haul longer trains. Various options were considered, but the front-runner was a 5,850-hp, 125-mph machine, which would work with Mark III coaches and a driving trailer. A prototype – 89001 – was built jointly by Brush Traction and British Rail Engineering Ltd, but by the time it appeared in 1986, InterCity director Dr John Prideaux – mindful that BR's reputation rested largely on InterCity's performance – had decided that 140mph was needed. This led to the 6,000hp GEC-built Class 91, with which came new Mark IV carriages and a new name: the InterCity 225. This – while a nod to the fact that 140mph is 225kmh – also helped create distance from the APT and an affinity with its more successful diesel-powered predecessor.

Like nationalisation, modernisation and rationalisation, sectorisation brought some of the biggest post-war changes to the railway. True, the new liveries often helped hide an ageing fleet, but Reid's efforts to win investment cash, coupled with continuing subsidiary sell-offs, land sales, staff reductions and an increasing use of computers for ticketing and delay monitoring, would see BR's finances start to shape up, as the losses of InterCity and Network SouthEast began to fall. (InterCity's loss of £99 million in 1986/87, for example, would shrink to £86 million in 1987/88, and become a surplus of £57 million in 1988/89.)

On the down side, BR had lost an estimated £250 million during the year-long miners' strike of 1984-5, £70 million of which was the result of the National Union of Railwaymen blacking the movement of coal (oil and iron ore were also affected). In addition, Parcels' £3 million surplus in 1986/87 became a £7 million loss in 1987/88 and a loss of £12 million in 1988/89, thanks to News International's contract-breaking withdrawal from rail (which led to the end of all newspaper traffic by July 1988), and the Royal Mail's decision to transfer more of its operation to other modes.

It was the same for the Speedlink freight service, whose salesmen were winning business ever further from the core network, meaning that the cost of tripping wagons from main yard to customer began to outstrip income. Its resemblance to the small-consignment wagonload operation it was meant to replace made the 1988 amalgamation with container-carrying Freightliner inevitable. Yet for this new company – Railfreight Distribution – hope came in the form of new business via the Channel Tunnel – a Victorian idea supported by BR in the 1970s, cancelled by Whitehall, rekindled by Parker, and finally ratified by the British and French governments in 1986.

As the decade drew to a close, work would be well under way on this impressive project, and what with the redevelopment of London Liverpool Street, East Coast electrification, increasing productivity, more stations, rising passenger numbers and falling subsidies, it seemed that sectorisation *was* working, that a golden age for BR really *was* dawning.

It was around this time that resignalling schemes had also been authorised or completed at Brighton, Newcastle, York, Leeds, Leicester, London Victoria and London Waterloo. The Waterloo Area Resignalling Scheme (WARS) was a particularly big operation, involving the replacement of equipment on the busiest stretch of railway in Britain, some 2,000 trains a day entering and leaving its sections, passing it or being held at its signals. It was a job-and-a-half and then some; a massive challenge, and a great responsibility that would bring the 1930s into the 1980s. It would also reduce the failure rate of the ageing equipment, cutting the risk of a signal showing green when it should in fact be red...

Chapter 7

Forging Ahead

Old Lights for New Chancels.
                    Title of John Betjeman poetry collection, 1940

Standing at Weymouth on a warm August day, the unmistakable yellow front of a 'Crompton' comes into view. Since 1967, these beasts had blasted in and out of Bournemouth with the Weymouth portions of trains from Waterloo. Now, in 1985, the Weymouth station of the Thirties is making way for a new one for the Nineties. Platform 3 has already gone, so the train snakes across to one of the old excursion bays. Its doors start to open. Some of the passengers – obviously used to commuting into the capital – jump down before it comes to rest; others, bound for hotels on the Esplanade, have too much luggage for any of that over-energetic stuff … though popping across to The Somerset for a quick one might not be a bad idea…

On the platform opposite, two boys sit with notebooks, cameras, cans of pop. Watching trains was still a popular pastime and would remain reasonably free from ridicule for a few more years. To the older one, the loco is a 6500, a Type 3; the younger one thinks more of its more recent Class 33 appellation. The latter will like the modern red brick building coming soon, will like even more the united colours of Network SouthEast, due to arrive a bit further on, due to be splashed across the cover of *Rail Enthusiast*'s August 1986 edition. But both may well lament the coming of the third rail and what it will mean for the trusty old diesels.

In electrifying the last 32 miles of the South Western Main Line, British Rail was both shoring up the 'crumbling edge' and carrying on the work so readily pursued by Sir Herbert Walker's Southern. Before the new railway, though, came that new station. Officially opened on 3 July 1986, it was the first one, other than Waterloo, to display the NSE slogan. The local councillor, David Hall, was there; the Mayor of Weymouth and Portland was there; Southern Region General Manager Gordon Pettitt was there. Pettitt was particularly delighted that the work had been completed on time, though as he said, it was 'just a start' where BR's investment in this part of the region was concerned.

Pettitt was referring to electrification, the news having broken a couple of months before that the government had approved the £43.5 million plan to bring it to the Dorset coast. It had not been easy to gain government approval, but it never was; at the other end of the line, work on WARS was marching on, but – signed off in December 1984 – it had first been mooted back in 1978! We will come back to this long lead time in Chapter 16, but for now note that Pettitt was a realist, who recognised that – at Weymouth at least – there was no way BR 'could have funded the cost of the station from increased passenger business'. Thankfully, the local authority had been 'very helpful in allowing [the Board] to develop unwanted railway land, to help meet the cost', as was evident in the way the old station's extensive platforms and yard were succumbing to modern commercial development.

Despite the new Weymouth, new buildings at Poole and Wareham, new signalling and platform lengthenings at Wool and Upwey, most of the scheme's cost involved new rolling stock. Ordered once approval had come, by the end of the year staff at Derby's Litchurch Lane works were considering plans for the twenty-four five-car electric units needed for the new service. And a new service it was certainly going to be, BR having realised that, although its commuter catchment in the Bournemouth area had expanded to stretch from Brockenhurst to Poole, locals were finding it hard to get through the pine-treed resort by road. It was clear that electrification could improve the timetable and allow NSE to offer a competitive 'swift and efficient cross conurbation service'.

But if the station was on time, the third rail being laid and the substations being erected, the trains themselves were a little behind. Deliveries had originally been expected from May 1987, but the first wasn't unveiled until 18 December. They were, perhaps, worth waiting for. *Rail Enthusiast* called them 'one of the most stylish new generation trains'; Chris Green called them 'our top of the range unit, our Ford Scorpio'. Indeed, and if any commuter had ever found the REPs noisy and unpleasant, the same could not be said of the 442s. Unlike their earlier brethren, they were asbestos free; unlike their earlier brethren, they were air conditioned; like them though, they featured corridors and compartments, or at least they did in First Class, where passengers could recline on a modish, red-striped seat with *The Times* or marvel at the mural art of Edward Pond (who was plain old Eddie Pond in Standard). By 1988, there was no BTF to herald the new arrivals, but it's not hard to imagine *Power to Portland* (or some similarly alliterative title) showing a suited gent getting up from a full (but not over-full) compartment, walking along the corridor in quiet comfort to make a phone call on the card-operated telephone, or get a coffee from the elegant buffet. While showing the gent – and probably a young family – enjoying the similar step-change in quality that Glasgow-Edinburgh passengers had been enjoying since 1979, and that Southern Region passengers were enjoying for the very first time, the film might also demonstrate how to operate the push-button plug doors, which were a lot safer than their HST or loco-hauled counterparts.

The irony is that these units – so much better than the REPs – in fact relied on the REPs, their traction motors and electrical control gear having been salvaged from them, albeit with the addition of new drive gearwheels and pinions. Either way, the combination of power train and aerodynamic design made the 442s fast. And – once the line had been fully energised – that speed could be demonstrated.

So to April. So to the 14th and Waterloo station. Departure time comes; a green light shines, a guard's whistle blows and a green flag waves. Imagine being a civic dignitary from Portland, taking your place in one of the ten red-white-and-blue coaches as the drivers, Bournemouth men Jim Gardiner and Alan Condon, take theirs in the cab. As they prepare for the off, you sit back in your compartment and light another Embassy. Soon, units 401 and 403 will snake over the pointwork and out onto plain line, passing Vauxhall, the site of the old Nine Elms depot, Clapham Junction, Raynes Park, Weybridge, Woking and Winchester. Soon you'll be beyond Bournemouth, beyond Branksome and heading for Wareham, Wool and Weymouth. By the time you step onto the platform to the sound of the Oakmead School Band less than two hours later, there'll have been a record-breaking top speed of 109mph on the descent into Winchester, an impressive average of 71.7 and an understanding that the future of rail travel on the old South Western was bright. Walker would have been pleased; Pettitt certainly *was* pleased, though not so pleased perhaps that only four units were available for the launch of the new timetable the following month, Derby having been held up by late component deliveries. Writing in *Rail Enthusiast*, Brian Perren felt moved to quote Fiennes, who himself had written that 'we on BR measure our delays in minutes but our suppliers measure [them] in months.'

What was a pain for the operating department, though, would have been pleasure for our two spotters as old Mark I trailer sets found themselves powered by pairs of Class 73s, so many REPs having been withdrawn to give up their innards for the new breed. Still, as the year wore on, more and more of these ground-breaking trains began to appear at Bournemouth Depot. They plied their trade without issue until 11 December, when unit 417 – working the 17:30 from Waterloo – struck a cement mixer left on the line near Parkstone. It derailed. It blocked the line. It meant the 06:14 from Poole would have to start from Bournemouth the following morning.

PART 2:

THE ELEMENTS COMBINE

Chapter 8

12 December 1988

All streets in time are visited.

Philip Larkin, *Ambulances*, 1964

Monday morning. Monday morning and at Bournemouth Depot, Driver John Rolls was signing on for duty. No reason why this Monday should be any different from any other Monday. Except for the incident last night, of course. Stupid kids! (If it *was* kids.) Fancy putting a bloody cement mixer on the line. Did for one of the new trains too!

But so it happened, and so it was that Rolls's first turn – 1B08, the 06:14 – would not be seeing the curved platform of Poole that morning. Soon after booking on, he took his 12-car formation out of the depot, over the points and into Branksome station, where he shut down and walked past the trailer cars to the REP at the London end. By the time he'd got there, the route had been set for him to run into Bournemouth. With an 06:30 departure, Rolls was soon powering his passengers on towards Southampton, the New Forest, all those places lauded in *Speedrail to the South*. Bournemouth's grand station roof had been damaged in the violent storms of October 1987, but thankfully the only storm today was a storm in a teacup when the guard, Paul Haywood, dropped his ticket clippers onto the track at Winchester.[10] There he let them stay while he stayed in his van and his passengers lost themselves in their own private worlds. Some contemplated news of an air crash in Armenia, some enjoyed the isolation afforded by their Walkmans, whether bringing Beatles, Beethoven, Bros or Bomb the Bass; others were doubtless contemplating Sartre.

Further forward, 2L10, the 07:18 ex-Basingstoke was also powering along, as the packed postal districts of London grew nearer and nearer. Like Haywood, Guard Fritsche stayed in his van, it becoming clear after Woking that the train was too busy for him to force his way through to check all the tickets. It was the usual story, for the 07:18 was usually full, its passengers too being lost in conversation, morning papers, novels, thoughts … Beyond Woking, the train passed through Surbiton, New Malden, Raynes Park, Wimbledon. It was cantering along at around 60mph when it approached WF138, a new signal commissioned on 27 November as part of the resignalling scheme so badly needed. The driver, Alexander McClymont, saw it was green, and got the 'bell and black disc' to confirm it. When the train was around 30 yards away, however, the aspect changed from green to red.[11] Something was wrong, and McClymont knew it. He rammed on the brakes, but then realised he'd be brought up short of WF47 signal, where he'd need to climb down and call the signaller. So he coasted, stopped, and made the call – to Clapham 'A'.

The phone was picked up by Patrick Cotter, who told McClymont that the indications in his box suggested there to be nothing wrong with WF138. By this time – just after eight – Rolls was bringing 1B08 closer to the cutting where the signal stood. On board, the crowded commuters continued with their conversations, their morning papers, novels, thoughts ... Green light followed green light: the usual story, yes – except the last one should have been red. As the train rounded the curve into the cutting, Rolls saw McClymont's train blocking the line ahead. He applied the emergency brake, but it was too late. The collision forced his leading coach to the side, where it struck 5P21, an empty unit passing on the opposite line, killing conversations ... thoughts ... and 33 people, among them Rolls himself, Alison McGregor, a keen sailor from Wimborne, and Michael Newman, a designer who'd worked for a number of West End theatres. Two more would succumb to their injuries later in hospital, including Bill Webb, a 39-year-old accountant, who'd been on his way to a new job in London, and whose daughter's birthday party had had to go ahead without him.

All the dead had been in the front two carriages, which had been ripped open down their left-hand sides. Of the 484 injured, 69 had been seriously hurt. Many had been trapped in and beneath the mass of twisted metal.

Ronald Arlette, who'd been on the 'Basingstoke', told *The Times* that there'd been 'an almighty bang, like an explosion. We went up and we flew over and over. We ended up on an embankment'. 'I know it sounds strange,' he added. 'But we just lay there and we had a laugh and a bit of a joke with each other. It just seemed the best thing to do to keep our spirits up.' Yet despite the resolve of some, there was terror, there was fear, there was dread. Mark Barthel, who'd been on the 'Poole', described how a man sitting in front of him 'died instantly in the impact', and how another man who'd been 'standing in the gap between the first and second carriages' was 'crushed to death'. Writing 25 years after the accident, journalist Paul Clifton recounted how one passenger later suffered post-traumatic stress disorder, leading him to excessive drinking. He lost his business, his house and those he loved.

News footage showed the bloodied faces, the shoulders shrouded in red blankets, the cramped conditions of rescue. BBC Radio 4 reported that the police used driving licences, cheque books, Christmas cards – the chattels of everyday life – to identify the victims. Jim MacMillan, Assistant Chief Officer of the London Fire Brigade, would call the scene 'sheer bloody hell'. Few would have disagreed – among them

McClymont, who'd been annoyed by Cotter's attitude, but when he heard the rending crash, when he saw his own train pushed forward several feet in front of him, picked up the receiver he'd only just put down and called again, told Cotter that something definitely *was* wrong, told him that casualties were now involved. Cotter threw all his signals back and sent the emergency ('six bells') code to his neighbouring boxes.[12] At the same time, the alarms went off at Raynes Park Electrical Control Room, where the Operator, Ronald Reeves, quickly switched off the current to the relevant sections.[13] This caused 2Y52, the 06:35 Waterloo, to lose power.[14] Its driver – Barry Pike – thought there might be a failure on board his train and decided to let it roll into Clapham Junction. It passed a green, it passed a double yellow and was then approaching WF138. As it neared the signal, Pike saw the wreckage, but was able to bring the train to a stand some 190 feet from it.

He went back to WF138 and phoned Cotter, telling him that the signal was now at yellow. Cotter said it should be red. 'Red aspect be damned,' said Pike. 'There are three trains standing in front of it, and it's still showing one yellow.'[15] The indications were wrong, and the problem wasn't far away.

In fact, it was in the relay room next to Clapham 'A'.

Chapter 9

Down to the Wire

New Bats in Old Belfries.
Title of John Betjeman poetry collection, 1945

The first to reach the scene had included the youngest, in the form of pupils from the nearby Emanuel School. Among them was Terry Stoppani, who'd turned twelve that day, and who had been walking along with his mates when the collision came. He told *The Times* of the train, of the people 'flying into the air', of how he started to help them to safety.

Terry, his fellow pupils and teachers would soon be joined by the emergency services, soon be joined by Gordon Pettitt, BR Director of Safety Maurice Holmes and the chairman himself, Sir Robert Reid. By lunchtime, the last living casualty had been removed from the wreckage;[16] by lunchtime Reid had accepted full responsibility on behalf of the organisation with honesty, dignity and professionalism. Pettitt would later say that the crash site was 'a view that you'd never forget, [that] the tangled mess of wreckage was unbelievable [and that the death toll was] shocking'.[17] Reid would later tell a colleague that Clapham 'was as much my fault as anyone's', that he felt he 'put pressure on people', and that he worried he might sometimes overdo it.[18] For now, he offered his and the Board's 'deepest sympathy to the families and friends of those who died' and wished 'a speedy recovery' to those who'd been injured.[19] He also pointed out that, while the government had called for a public inquiry, BR's investigators had already launched their own. Within ten hours, they had established many of the facts. An official statement said the 'probable cause' had been 'a technical fault following preparatory work in connection with the Waterloo resignalling scheme,' adding that 'claims for compensation [would] be considered sympathetically and as quickly as possible'.

As the names of the dead became known, the Board members wrote to each family, expressing regret and offering help, including immediate payments of £2,000 to next of kin, and the settlement of funeral expenses. They also wrote to the injured, visited them in hospital and offered to meet travel and other expenses for visiting relatives, 'particularly if the injured [were] in hospital over the Christmas holiday'.

If ever a Christmas took an age to come, it took an age that year. And what thoughts of injustice might have been on the minds of managers as Advent ebbed away? It had, after all, been one of the safest years the railway had ever seen…until that bright-dark December Monday morning.[20] By the Friday, Holmes had confirmed the Board's preliminary findings – that the signalling equipment where the collision occurred 'had been defectively installed [and] that the defective installation [had] interfered with the fail-safe systems of that stretch of line'.[21]

This was three days into the inquiry, which had been convened at Waterloo on the Wednesday, and would see 34 witnesses by Tuesday 20th. Four men formed the panel: Holmes naturally took the chair; with him were Ken Hodgson (Director of Signal & Telecommunications), Jim Vine (Mechanical & Electrical Engineer) and Alan Galley, Regional Operations Manager of the Southern Region.[22] Almost immediately – just three pages in – their report homes in on the events of 26 and 27 November, when a number of track circuits were converted to a jointless type designed to eliminate failures, and a number of new signals – including WF138 – were commissioned.[23] On the 27th, the Sunday, Supervisor Derek Bumstead was in charge of the changeover of wiring in the Clapham 'A' relay room, which was to be undertaken by Senior Technician Brian Hemingway and Technician Patrick Dowd.[24] Part of the job – Job 111 – was to convert track circuit DM to a jointless type, and part of *that* involved dealing with a black wire connecting its relay to the fuse and terminal board.[25] The report describes how Hemingway marked the diagram with a pencil tick for each wire connected and a cross for each one removed, but points out that he 'suffered an unusual number of unplanned interruptions whilst carrying out this task, which put the work well behind schedule'. In the event, he did not clip off the eye of the wire and neither insulated it with tape nor disconnected the other end (a safe alternative to total removal, which reduced the chance of disturbing the embrittled coverings on other adjoining wires).[26] He also didn't carry out a wire count, which would have detected the wire; but then neither had Bumstead, who felt it could be done after commissioning.[27]

At first, the wire wasn't making contact, and as the functional test carried out by Acting Testing and Commissioning Engineer Peter Dray showed everything to be working as it should, the latter signed the equipment back into work.[28] All was well.

All was not well. Two weeks later, on Sunday 11 December, three more track circuits were scheduled for conversion. The relay for track circuit DN was right next to the one for track circuit DM. Hemingway was doing the work again. He made the changeover 'in difficult, cramped conditions' made worse by the amount of redundant wiring and equipment left in place after various modifications down the years, made worse still by poor lighting, there having been no natural light in the relay room, only fluorescent lighting from the ceiling. Fluorescent lights do not render colours as accurately as natural light, so it's easy to imagine how difficult it must have been trying to look at the diagram to discern colour codes and one's own pencil marks under those circumstances. And it was under those circumstances – all of them – that the black wire on track circuit DM's relay reverted to the natural position it had held for many years and 'came into contact with the terminal to which it was originally connected'.[29] A <u>wrong-side failure</u> was suddenly inevitable.

Chapter 10

Changing Tides

You just can't get the staff.

Traditional

Signal Maintenance Engineer Ian Harman was on the phone in his Wimbledon office, talking to his assistant at Feltham, when the alarm sounded on the operating floor.[30] The assistant rang off to find out what had happened. The news was not good. Harman went straight to site, where he saw the carnage for himself, where he was told of McClymont's change of aspect.

At this point, WF138 was showing a cautioning single yellow. Harman opened the location cabinet and saw that the relay was energised. It should not have been. He adjusted it to turn the signal red and made his way back to Clapham 'A', where he checked the relay circuit for WF138 to the record of what Hemingway had done on 27 November. On terminal 4A, there were two wires – the old black one and a new blue one. Closer inspection revealed that while the former was not connected to the terminal, its metal eye was touching. It was of course the eye Hemingway should have clipped off, and it meant that – for Rolls – green light really had followed green light until the collision came (a fact confirmed by a chart in the BRB report which showed the probable headway for the Up Main between 08:05 and 08:15 and the green aspect at WF138 as Rolls passed it).[31]

In trying to make things better, things had been made worse.[32] But it didn't stop there: after the accident, the errant wire was 'removed, the eye cut off and the end taped up'. This removed the supply of current to the WF138 HR relay, but also removed vital evidence from the scene without so much as a photograph having been taken for the investigation. The BRB report noted this, recounted too how colour-light signalling had come to the route in 1936.[33] As we saw, it and the electric interlocking that extended from Waterloo had been part of Sir Herbert Walker's modernisation drive for the Southern Railway. It had helped that company increase the numbers of trains it could run and the passengers it could carry. Within forty years, though, the wiring – especially at Waterloo signal box – was starting to show 'signs of becoming brittle'.[34]

What once was new, perforce grows old, and 'after several false starts, authority [had been] obtained in 1982 for the renewal of the interlocking (only) at Waterloo Station'.[35] By the time the work had been commissioned in February 1984, however, it had become Stage 1 of the whole Waterloo Area Resignalling Scheme. WARS was a huge project, a huge change to the railway. Like all such changes, a great deal of preliminary work had had to be done to make sure the final arrangement was achieved 'as safely and as quickly as possible'.[36] ML Engineering of Plymouth had provided the design; British Rail was duly implementing it. Stage 7 took in Clapham Junction and was destined to be the first section controlled from a new signalling centre at Wimbledon.[37] It had been in progress since 1986. Pressure from BR's sectors to minimise the length of time a line was blocked to traffic meant mainly weekend work and involved 'phasing in' the new signalling to a plan that the Signal Engineer (Works) at the Project Office in Croydon had formed around the requirements of the Area Signal Engineer (Works) at the Signal & Telecommunications (S&T) Engineer's office in Wimbledon. From this, a set of numbered wiring diagrams had been produced, which were then passed to the S&T Engineer responsible for getting the job done.[38]

A roster was drawn up to show when each task was to be performed, and by whom.[39] Dray, as Acting Testing and Commissioning Engineer, then discussed specific jobs with specific supervisors. This is how Bumstead came to be responsible for the work undertaken inside and outside Clapham 'A' on 27 November, and how Hemingway came to be on his day shift, which consisted of 12 staff, plus a supervisor on loan from another section.[40] For the 'inside work' on 11 December, however, Hemingway had fulfilled the 'triple role' of Senior Technician, supervisor, *and* tester, thereby 'negating an independent check of the work'.[41]

The requirement for an independent check was outlined in BR's Southern Region Instruction SL-53, *Testing of New and Altered Signalling*, which aimed to move away from the 'learn by observation' pattern of old, and which specified that, for 'line fuse terminations' like Job 111, a 'wire count [should be carried out] on all free wired safety relays and terminations', and that a record should be made 'on the contact/terminal analysis sheets'.[42] It also specified that a continuity test should be made to check that each wire was connected to the correct terminal, and that a functional test should be made to check that the signals, pointwork and train detection circuits were working as designed.[43] Instruction SI-16, *Termination of Signalling Cables and Wires*, added that 'wires and crimps not terminated must have their ends insulated and secured to prevent contact with each other or any other equipment'. Hemingway wasn't sure if he had a copy, though it was clear he hadn't complied with it.[44]

Part of the problem involved reorganisation and staffing. Before May 1988, the Southern's S&T function had centred on East Croydon. In April, though, responsibility for development and design had been transferred to the Director of S&T Engineering, based at the Board's Macmillan House headquarters in Paddington. *At the same time*, responsibility for construction passed to three new Area S&T

Engineers, one of whom was based at Wimbledon. The latter took on the responsibility for testing and commissioning new works. *At the same time*, the closure of the depots at South Lambeth and New Cross Gate meant that staff from both 'formed the nucleus of the Works team created at Wimbledon'.[45] That's a lot of reorganisation in a small window of time, and it explains how some managers found themselves without job descriptions for the posts they occupied.[46] As to Hemingway doing three jobs on 11 December, Wimbledon simply couldn't get the staff, a concurrent drop in staffing levels having created a 'high level of vacancies', some of which had been filled by people coming in 'on loan' from other depots, some of which had been filled by people 'displaced' by the reorganisation, some of which had not been filled at all.[47] Those 'on loan' were unknown quantities, not perhaps to be trusted implicitly with important work; the 'displaced' included people with low levels of motivation and job satisfaction. Dray was among this second group, having been uprooted from his post as Senior Engineer (Works) at Ashford.[48]

The report's conclusions made no mention of the reorganisation and its effects, focussing mainly on the precise errors of 27 November and 11 December, and noting that the ultimate responsibility for the accident 'must be shared by the Line Management of the Area S&T E[ngineering] organisation at Wimbledon, who [were] accountable for the arrangements made for the site work, ensuring the correct allocation of staff and accountabilities, also that procedures to secure the safety of the signalling installation [were] adhered to.'[49]

The recommendations that followed – and the appendices that followed them – hinted at the wider problems that led to Clapham, but by the time the report had been released on 23 December, the public inquiry that would expand on the themes revealed by BR was already well under way.

Chapter 11

Enter Hidden

Out of this nettle, danger, we pluck this flower, safety.

Shakespeare,

Henry IV, part 1

At around half-past three on the afternoon of 12 December, Secretary of State for Transport, MP for Southend West and erstwhile Secretary of State for Trade and Industry, Paul Channon addressed the House of Commons. Being a transport minister was something of a thankless task. Thankless and short-lived; since 1960, there had been fifteen with rail responsibilities. Sometimes, disapprobation came with the announcement of funding cuts – or increases, if there were louder calls for cash elsewhere; sometimes though it was their sad duty to announce tragedy. And Channon's was a tenure destined to be blighted thus. Soon after he'd taken the mantle the year before, the King's Cross tube station fire had taken 31 lives; the Lockerbie air disaster would take 270 more in the short days ahead. This afternoon, though, his mind could only be on Clapham.

Channon had visited the crash site that morning, had seen the scene of death and destruction for himself. He said BR was already investigating, praised their recent safety record, praised the emergency services too. He also announced his intention 'to appoint an inspector to conduct a full independent inquiry into the accident, in public, under the provisions of the Regulation of Railways Act 1871'.[50] For *Times* journalist Matthew Parris, observing the scene for his regular 'political sketch', Channon had not the 'self-importance which can make expressions of regret from so many politicians sound hollow'. Indeed, his distress 'as he rose to give his statement, was evident'. He looked 'weary and sad', speaking briefly and factually, refusing to be drawn by 'a few rather ill-judged attempts to anticipate the inquiry's conclusions'.

Time would prove that not *all* these attempts, these questions, were ill judged. Some indeed were very pertinent and would pick up on themes that the forthcoming inquiry would root out. For the time being, though, Channon reiterated that the inquiry would not 'dodge getting to the bottom of what occurred … so that the appropriate lessons can be learned'.[51] The following day, he appointed barrister and Queen's Counsel Anthony Hidden to lead the proceedings. Stanley Hall, former Head of Signalling and Accidents at BR HQ, would later blame 'intense media interest' and 'political pressure from [Channon's] parliamentary shadow [John Prescott]' for this 'over-hasty reaction'.[52] But – as BR's official historian Terry Gourvish would note – Clapham, King's Cross and Lockerbie were not the only disasters suffered in this era; there was also the *Herald of Free Enterprise*, which capsized near Zeebrugge in March 1987 with the loss of 193 lives; and the *Piper Alpha* oil rig explosion, which killed 167 in July 1988. For Gourvish, this was therefore a period of 'enhanced public scrutiny', not only of railway safety, but of safety in general. Hardly surprising, then, that Channon would call for an inquiry to satisfy that scrutiny, although as it turned out there was probably less choice in the matter than it might have appeared.

Section 7 of the 1871 Act allowed the government to direct a 'county court judge, stipendiary magistrate, metropolitan police magistrate, or

other person or persons named in the same or any subsequent order'
to conduct 'a more formal investigation' of an incident above the order
of the more usual Railway Inspectorate inquiry, if deemed 'expedient'.
There had been two other inquiries into main line rail accidents since
the passing of the Act. In both cases, that 'expediency' had centred on
the fact that the Railway Inspectorate had been compromised in terms
of its requisite impartiality. The Tay Bridge disaster had been the first,
because the RI had been involved in the bridge's approval. Over 70
people had been killed by its collapse on 28 December 1879. Hixon
had been next, the RI having been involved in the approval process for
<u>automatic half-barrier crossings</u>, which had played a large part in the
collision that killed 11 people at the start of 1968.

In fact, the RI had been overseeing WARS too – only partially,
although the role it had, or should have had, was confused by the
somewhat ambiguous Road and Rail Traffic Act 1933, which had
attempted to clarify which 'classes of new work on the railway' required
the Secretary of State for Transport's approval. There had been a bid to
iron out the ambiguity in 1958, but as Hidden would note, even the
resulting 'administrative letter' still had *some* ambiguity about it. Thirty
years later, this created a situation in which the RI was aware that WARS
was being carried out, but had received a submission to consider only
two parts of the work. Both had been approved and inspected after
commissioning, which made it seem as though the RI had condoned
the non-submission of the rest. Yet even if this had *not* been the case,
it had no mechanism to force the timely submission of the whole
scheme. Arguably, all this put the RI in 'an extremely difficult position'.
Arguably, a public inquiry it *had* to be.

The formal hearings began on 20 February 1989 and received
evidence from 122 witnesses over the following 56 days. By then, there'd
been two further accidents, both fatal, both resulting from signals being

passed at danger. On 4 March 1989, a passenger train struck another at Purley in South London, killing five people and injuring 88. Two days later, another train struck an incoming service at Bellgrove Junction, near Glasgow; this time, the driver and a passenger were killed, with 53 reported hurt. It was decided that, although Clapham was *not* a SPAD, the inquiry would also look at any common issues that arose from all three incidents.

Hidden would write that his prime purpose was 'to seek to establish both the immediate and the underlying causes' of Clapham. BR had beaten him to the former, but his report would clarify the elements that combined to create the latter.

Chapter 12

Writing the Wrongs

Leave no rubs nor botches in the work.

Shakespeare,
Macbeth

Back in the House on Tuesday 7 November 1989, a newer Secretary of State for Transport took up a slightly older theme. Cecil Parkinson had taken over from Paul Channon in July, a warmer time that had turned colder as the year began to ebb. At around half-three that afternoon, he rose and told the assembly he was about to publish 'the results of the inquiry into the Clapham Junction rail disaster'. Hidden had signed off his report on 27 September; now was the time for it to be shared.

Parkinson reiterated everyone's regrets, everyone's thanks to those who acted with skill, courage and kindness that day almost a year before. He outlined the immediate cause, noted how there had been 'major defects' in the way BR had organised WARS, and added that Hidden had made 93 recommendations, some of which were aimed at preventing a recurrence, some of which were intended to secure 'improvements in [BR's] management and organisational systems for safety', some of which were directed to the emergency services and the government itself.

The report started like most reports of its kind, by going through the procedural history, describing what had been asked for, by whom, and who had assisted. Hidden noted that he'd been aided by three Assessors: Major Christopher Holden (Inspecting Officer of Railways); Dr Bryce McCrirrick (President of the Institution of Electrical Engineers); and Dr Alan Wells (former Director General of the Welding Institute). He said he had tried to remain mindful of 'the dangers of using the powerful beam of hindsight to illuminate the situations revealed in the evidence'. Instead, he began to paint an ever-clearing picture of what had happened on 12 December 1988 – and why.

For Hidden, there were essentially three questions to consider. The first – *how had the accident happened?* – had been answered by BR: the signalling system had failed. The second – *how had the signalling system failed?* – had also been answered by BR: Hemingway had left a wire in place that was able to revert to 'the natural position it had held over many years'. This allowed it to touch a terminal, make a connection and prevent WF138 signal from returning to danger after the passage of McClymont's train. Hidden paid tribute to the 'care, skill and expertise' which went into BR's report, 'and to the speed and diligence which made it available so early'.

The final question – *how had that situation been allowed to happen?* – was of course the hardest to answer, and the one that formed the rest of the report. Thus after dealing with the accident itself, the response to it and Hemingway's errors, Hidden came to how those errors were made.[53]

At the time, Hemingway had been with BR for sixteen years, and had been a Senior Technician Scale A since January 1981. He had ten years of experience in electrical installation, having worked on large resignalling schemes at both London Bridge and Victoria. He was held 'in high regard by his colleagues and his superiors'. He was proud of his work, and told the inquiry that, on the morning of 27 November 1988, he had felt the way he always felt: 'alright'.

Hemingway's assistant that day, as BR had noted, had been Patrick Dowd, who had also joined BR in 1972. The pair had worked together on two or three previous weekends, but Hemingway was uncomfortable with having Dowd as his assistant; Dowd's hands 'shook too much' for his liking. As a result, Hemingway decided to take on most of the work himself, although there had been no question of anyone 'putting pressure on him to work quicker than he could properly and safely [have done]'. He said he had not expected anyone to check his work that day, as he was basically working on his own, partly because he had shunned support from Dowd and partly because the designated supervisor, Bumstead, was working 'long and hard' outside with a track gang ('often carrying out the manual work himself'). This was in some ways laudable, but in 'fulfilling the role of a senior technician rather than a supervisor', wrote Hidden, Bumstead had 'totally neglected his duties as a supervisor'. Indeed, he did not enter the relay room at all that day.

In *Hidden Dangers*, Stanley Hall commented that Bumstead's actions tallied with 'most departments throughout the railway industry since World War 2', something that was 'particularly bad in the London area'. The important role supervisors played 'in ensuring that jobs were done and that the railway continued to function can only be fully appreciated by someone who experienced it,' he went on. Managers were 'reluctant to admit that the practice existed, but they accepted the situation because they recognised that circumstances gave them no alternative'. Nevertheless, in this case, Hemingway *was* left under-supervised; he was also, in Hidden's estimation, under-trained.

It was not as though Hemingway had passed no courses at all. In fact, he had passed several, including a preliminary course of seven weeks, a basic signalling course of four weeks, a couple of short courses at the Derby Training School and a course on level crossing equipment.[54]

Yet he had risen to the rank of Senior Technician not by passing an examination, but because of a 'change in staffing arrangements'; a 1974 'pay and grading' agreement brought the need to pass exams en route to progression, but Hemingway had been in the S&T Department for enough time to be 'allowed to regrade without taking the [requisite] courses'. Hence Hidden's opinion that 'he had a *bare minimum* of training' and '*no training for any technical qualification* whatever' (author's italics). Hidden records that this exacerbated a number of poor working practices that Hemingway 'had been making all his working life', namely never cutting old wires back, never tying them back and never insulating the bare ends with new insulating tape (preferring to re-use pre-used tape instead). Worse still, these errors were endemic, were 'part of a widespread way of working' within the Southern Region's S&T Department, despite the existence of instruction SI-16 (*Termination of Signalling Cables and Wires*).

Coupled with these 'characteristic' errors, alas, were a number of 'uncharacteristic' ones, such as leaving the old black wire connected at the fuse end and not insulating the bare end at all (with new tape, pre-used tape or anything else). For all this, Hidden does note Hemingway's meticulousness, in the sense that – whether his working practices were right or wrong – he followed them closely and consistently. How then could the so-called 'uncharacteristic' errors have been made? There were two strands to consider. First, there was an interruption. BR had already revealed there to have been an 'unusual number' that day, but as Hemingway told the public inquiry 'if it goes like normal I generally get interrupted. It goes like that'. One, though, came after he had moved the black wire, but before he could insulate it. The precise nature of that interruption could not be pinned down: Hemingway could recall Dowd bringing tea, someone from the outside team seeking help with a problem, others coming in to check drawings. He accepted that this could have caused him to make a mistake.

There was 'a moment of forgetfulness' in which Hemingway thought he had finished his morning's work. It was understandable – he nearly *had* finished – but also unusual. Hemingway was not 'a man prone to lapses of concentration'. But he was, according to Hidden, an honest man, who – when interviewed at the hearing – 'gave a series of very frank and objective answers without at any time seeking to excuse himself for his errors'. The series of exchanges ended with a very simple one:

> Q: You are certainly not seeking to blame tiredness or pressure of work yourself for the mistakes that occurred.
> A: No. Sir.

That said, Hemingway had, concluded Hidden, undertaken constant, repetitive work and excessive levels of overtime, both of which had 'blunted his working edge'. To be more explicit, he had had one day off in the previous 13 weeks. To a twenty-first century reader, this length of time seems incredible – foolhardy even. Current guidance notes that while 'there is no single scientific definition of fatigue', it is accepted that 'fatigue is generally a feeling of extreme tiredness and being unable to perform work effectively. It is a state of impairment that can result from prolonged working, heavy workload, insufficient rest and inadequate sleep and can include mental and/or physical elements'. Indeed, 'research suggests that people's awareness of feeling tired increases with increasing fatigue, then peaks, and then starts to reduce with extreme levels of fatigue. So people who are in a very fatigued state may say that they don't feel tired'.[55]

This would appear to be exactly the state Hemingway was in, yet back in 1988 it was part of the culture; back then, it was acceptable;

back then it was (for many) a financial necessity. Indeed, to work this time was Hemingway's own choice, for the weekend workforce was never selected, 'it ... selected itself', those wishing to work the weekends ticking the appropriate column on the appropriate sheet on their depot's noticeboard. Even today the question 'do you want to rest, or do you want to pay your mortgage?' is sometimes heard, but as BR had revealed, there was an eight-month-old baby in the Hemingway household. This meant a new-born to be provided for, but it also meant that Hemingway would not have been getting the best sleep either.[56]

Fatigued or not, no one was telling Hemingway he was taking too much overtime, no one was telling him that the way he dealt with old wires was wrong. No one, in short, was supervising him to any adequate extent at all.

Chapter 13

Supervision and Organisation

Quis custodiet ipsos custodes.
(Who guards the guards?)

Juvenal

The Sixteen Satires

From the most humble to the most arrogant of us, we all make mistakes. It is human. That is why, in safety critical work like resignalling a railway, there are a series of checks and inspections every step of the way. Hemingway's mistakes should have been picked up by proper supervision. His supervisor, Bumstead, chose to work outside on 27 November. He may have told the inquiry that he had expected Hemingway to do his own wire count, and that this had been 'the general practice for years'. Hidden may have pointed out that Bumstead's supervision had been wanting, but it was Testing and Commissioning Engineer Peter Dray with whom the buck stopped as far as the responsibility for testing was concerned.

Six weeks before, Dray had been working (and living) out of Ashford as Senior Signal Engineer (Works). Now he was working out of Wimbledon, his old job having disappeared in the mist of the May reorganisation. The BR report said his motivation had to be 'questioned', said that his 'job satisfaction was very low'.[57] Hidden would describe him as a man with 'little liking' for the job and 'less enthusiasm' for it. It's not hard to see why. Take the accident out of the equation and it's not hard to feel sympathy for Dray either; here was a man who had built a life for himself in one place and at the stroke of a pen was forced to travel the 70-odd miles into the capital to do a job about which he had been given no choice. Faced with a similar situation, would you say something like 'well, that's railways for you' and accept it as inevitable? Or would you resent the system and lament all the things you won't be able to do, the people you'll have to disappoint, the chores you won't feel like doing, even the television programmes you'll miss as you nod off in your chair night after night? All speculation of course, but there's no reason at all to think that anyone whose name appears in an accident inquiry report feels or thinks any differently from any of the rest of us – before that accident has occurred, at least.

Hidden clarified that Dray had applied for four or five other jobs after the May reorganisation, but had been successful in none. It must have been a very draining and soul-destroying process. Gordon Callander, the erstwhile Senior Construction Assistant at South Lambeth, became the Southern's South West Area Testing and Commissioning Engineer during the same restructuring. When he moved on again in October, though, Dray found himself taking the role on a temporary (six-week) basis. On paper, he was a good choice – as BR's report noted, he might not have been 'appointed permanently to the position', but he did have 'previous experience in the testing field'.

Previous experience? Maybe. Although the truth was that Dray had not performed a wire count for ten or eleven years. He had been back in blissful Ashford when an early, provisional set of instructions had come out in October 1985. He thought it was a discussion document and wrote a few comments on a scrap of paper. It had actually taken three years to prepare and issue, Regional S&T Engineer Clifford Hale having requested a formal set of testing instructions to be drafted towards the end of 1982. A letter sent in November 1985, written on

Hale's behalf, gave the document – 'SL-Provisional' – full authority, just like 'any other Departmental Instruction'. Paragraph 3.3 stated that '[a] wire count must be carried out on all free-wired safety relays and terminations and recorded on the contact/terminal analysis sheets.' Dray didn't get the letter. He therefore didn't realise that a wire count was now mandatory. He wasn't the only one who didn't get it; maybe he, maybe they, felt that anything labelled 'provisional' was just that. Either way, Dray, Hemingway and Bumstead all ended up thinking 'that any sort of wire count was no responsibility of theirs'. None of them understood 'the essential importance of an *independent* wire count' either (Hidden's italics). This attitude did not change when SL-53 (*Testing of New and Altered Signalling*) appeared in May 1987.

So much for Ashford, but when Dray got to Wimbledon, he entered a place where SL-53 was not being implemented at all. Callander said he 'did not regard it as significant enough' to tell Dray, but Dray never saw himself as the person in charge of testing, did not think himself of a 'high enough grade' to take charge of testing and made no attempt to put SL-53 into practice himself.

Of course, it didn't help that SL-53 was 'issued with no accompanying explanation by management, and no seminars or training in how it should be implemented'. Nor did it help that management did not *monitor* the implementation of SL-53, believing that it was being 'implemented in spirit'. This, said Hidden, was 'a pious hope'.

For his part, Dray felt he could do his job by performing the functional test alone (although he later admitted that this test did not 'ensure the safety of the equipment'). He also felt he should remain by the phone on the signalling floor of Clapham 'A', as 'people want to know where you are all the time' (although he knew he could have sent someone into the relay room to do the wire count for him on 27 November). For BR, Dray was 'under misapprehension as to his role'.[58] In fact, Dray had been given no induction training and, though he and Callander were both at Wimbledon before the latter left, 'they were doing different types of work and only saw each other on some mornings'. Callander's attitude to the job was damaged by the fact that he 'was not completely content' in his new role, having lost the planning part of his previous one. His attitude to Dray was damaged by the fact that Dray's appointment had not been permanent, meaning that Callander saw him as a mere 'caretaker'. As a result, he did not discuss Dray's duties in any detail, nor underline the fact that, under SL-53, it *would* be Dray's responsibility to make sure the wire count was carried out.

That Dray was roundly criticised was right on one level, but as Hidden wrote, this was 'not an isolated failure on the part of one man'. No, it was endemic throughout the whole S&T Department. Part of the problem here was that Callander did not like SL-53. When he'd first received a copy, he'd still been at South Lambeth. He knew it was an important document that needed to be read closely, but he simply had no time to study it. He had too much on, and he knew that, if he *had* read it, he would have 'decided he was incapable of carrying out all of the duties' anyway. His suspicions were not unfounded – SL-53 was ambiguous on the number of people required for testing on large commissions. Either way, he ignored it and hoped it would go away, an attitude he took with him to Wimbledon, where his technicians and supervisors were signing documents claiming to be compliant with it. And yet 'at no stage did any of [his] superiors enquire whether he was working to SL-53 or discover that he was not'.

Thus not only was the tester not testing according to Departmental Instructions, but the management was not managing the tester.

As we saw, Callander did not think it for him to be performing a wire count; Dray felt much the same thing, so whichever one of them had been Testing and Commissioning Engineer on 27 November would have made little difference to the dire outcome of 12 December. But what about the next level of management? Did the person on the next rung up from Callander feel any differently?

The person on that rung was Geoff Bailey. Before the reorganisation, Bailey had been the Regional Testing Engineer, in charge of the Regional Testing Team at Croydon. He moved to Wimbledon to take up the position of Signal Works Engineer and was actually in the relay room at Clapham 'A' on 27 November. And yet he had a self-admitted 'blind spot' on the subject of wire counts, despite believing the golden rule of testing to be 'to make sure the railways were safe for trains to run on'. In fact, and with some hindsight-fuelled irony, Bailey was in post to 'raise the standard of testing on the Region and particularly to attempt to avoid some of the failures that had occurred at or just after commissioning'. He was told this by the Regional S&T Engineer, Clifford Hale. But though Hale had 'expressed great concern' about these failures, he never told Bailey what they were, and never briefed him on how he was to go about raising standards. Bailey was just left to get on with it, with only two assistants and a large workload. This meant that, when he met with Callander to discuss the testing arrangements for WARS, he in turn left Callander to get on with it. Like Dray, Bailey got sight of SL-Provisional; like Dray he thought it was a consultation draft and – like Dray – made a few comments on it. He also drew up a testing check list … which did not refer to making wire counts. His boss, S&T Signal Engineer (Projects) Robert Davies, added a reference after it had been sent to him for review, but did not take it up with Bailey, thereby missing a chance to point out – in person – the importance of an independent wire count.

When SL-53 proper came into force, it was agreed at a meeting from which Bailey was absent that it would be implemented on a job at Forest

Hill, which was still in the future even from Hidden's standpoint. He received no instruction that SL–53 was in force and no instruction in its implementation (which was odd, given his role and what he was meant to be doing with it). He would admit at the public inquiry that the document had 'a greater significance to him than to any other individual in [the] Southern Region'. As Hidden wrote:

> It is a matter which the Court can only look upon with both alarm and horror (a word not usually suitable for the dispassionate analysis which is required for an Investigation such as this) that the man in overall charge of the testing of new works for the whole of [the] Southern Region could have arrived at a conclusion that a Departmental Instruction which had as its very title 'TESTING OF NEW AND ALTERED SIGNALLING' and had been formally and properly issued, was not in force, and that he could have persisted in that view for a period of one and a half years between the issue of that document and the accident.

Worse, Bailey was not working to SL–Provisional either, nor to good practice, *all* of which saw the need for a wire count. The blind spot Bailey admitted to had prevented him from improving the Region's testing in the manner Hale had wanted. As Hidden wrote, it 'almost beggars belief'.

Chapter 14

Claphams in the making

Learning without thought is labour lost; thought without learning is perilous.

Confucius, *Analects*

The story of what Hale had wanted began in 1985. At this time, new signalling was being commissioned between Sanderstead and Oxted, on the line to East Grinstead. Originally planned for 17 July, the work was postponed so some of the track circuits could be reduced to bring them into line with the lengths used in electrified areas elsewhere.[59] Contractors in railway work are nothing new, and it was Westinghouse Signals that had offered to design, supply, install and test the new scheme by the September of that year, with full commissioning to take place on 2 November.

The resource plan of the Signal Construction Engineer at New Cross Gate allowed five weeks for the necessary preparations to be completed. This was longer than usual, but the delay from July to November meant there was now a clash with remodelling work scheduled for Metropolitan Junction, between Waterloo East and London Bridge. This put more pressure on managers at New Cross Gate, particularly as the Design Office was not able to supply the staff needed to cover BR's obligation to design, check and test all the circuitry that linked the new equipment with the old, and to carry out the final functional testing to check that everything was working as it should.[60]

The project had extended the reach of the Area Signalling Centre at Three Bridges from Sanderstead to Upper Warlingham, beyond which a number of automatically signalled sections had been provided, monitored from Oxted Signal Box. The alterations required within the latter were not substantial and a lot of preparation had been able to be done in advance. If there was going to be a problem, everyone thought, it was going to be at the Sanderstead end. Staff were deployed with that in mind. The checking was pressured, the checking was tough – but it was done, and by Commissioning Day the railway was back in use. Except. Except that beneath the cool, blue surface of completion were ripples of error. The first that came to light came that same Monday morning, at Woldingham Ground Frame, a set of levers used to operate a trailing crossover not required in the normal run of traffic. During the re-signalling works, a supervisor attended the frame to fix a faulty set of 'lock proving' contacts. He made his repair and performed a functional test. The frame become effective immediately. There should have been a two-minute delay to allow the approach locking on the protecting signal to be released, so that the signal could be returned to danger. This delay should have been ensured by a timer. But there was no timer. The investigation revealed its absence to have resulted from a design error. A note of the deficiency had been made … but not shared with anyone else.

At 08:15 that morning, the signaller at Oxted thought an East Grinstead service was taking a devil of a time to pass through the section between Sanderstead and his box.[61] He was right – autumn leaf fall had created adhesion problems, causing the train to travel more slowly than usual. As a result, a following train (from Victoria) was brought to a stand at OD3 signal, just outside Woldingham station. At about 09:00, its driver called the box and said the signal had shown green, red and yellow aspects in succession. As a semi-automatic signal, OD3 would normally show yellow or green if the track circuit ahead was clear. However, that circuit was some 1,820 metres long. As a result, it had been reconfigured into three sections, in order to keep the length of each constituent section within the prescribed 820-metre maximum. Occupation of any of the three sections should have held OD3 at danger. Unfortunately, the middle one had not been wired correctly, meaning that the ex-Victoria was shown a proceed aspect at OD3 when it should have been red to protect the 'East Grinstead'. When the wiring changes were made, the only test Westinghouse did was to make sure the wiring matched the diagram.[62] BR accepted that all was as it should have been and therefore conducted a functional test and an aspect sequence test only, the latter using normal timetabled trains to operate the track circuits with a man at each signal, as there were not enough men to conduct a full and proper check via the track relays. The irregular signal sequence was missed, though, because 'the observer at OD3 was only monitoring the signal when asked to report its aspect'. In other words, he only looked when he was told.

The final Oxted incident was, for Hidden, 'the most alarming' as it involved a wrong-side failure in that a signal was 'allowed to show a green aspect when it should not have done'.[63] That signal, OD7, had two issues. First, a design error had allocated both contacts of a relay to different circuits as if they were independent.[64] Secondly, a torn instruction sheet led a redundant wire to be cut into a circuit when it should not have been. These two mistakes made a wrong-side failure a real possibility. Both could – *should* – have been discovered by a wire count, but – as with Clapham three years later – no such count had been undertaken, only a preliminary functional test on 30 October. The internal report noted that the wire count had not been done as 'it was being delayed until all recoveries had taken place'.[65] In part, this had been to save time, but, as the report clarified, wire counts were supposed to be carried out *immediately*.

Testing had always been the prestige job for S&T staff, a step on the path to management even. But now it seemed that there had been a 'movement towards greater reliance on contractors' own checking and testing', which had meant that 'large volumes of work' were passing unchecked by BR staff. This also seemed to facilitate 'a downwards drift in the standards of production and checking of BR's own work', which put 'greater and greater pressure on the functional tester', a breed dwindling in number thanks to a drop in staff and supervisors, whose work had been shifted 'upwards to the outside management staff'.[66]

In the wake of Oxted, Hale had chaired a Departmental Conference, at which it was minuted that 'instructions must be obeyed'; in the wake of Oxted, SL-Provisional was mandated with the instruction that wire counts must be carried out.[67] But Hale did not discuss this with Bailey, and though the Oxted papers were handed to him, Bailey 'never took on board their lessons'. Two further incidents occurred that same week – at Northfleet and East Croydon, the former occurring when a signaller noticed irregular aspects being shown by a signal, the latter leading to a side-on collision between two passenger trains.[68]

Alarm bells should have been ringing everywhere, but all that happened was a 'brief flurry of paperwork', which provided important information, but which was shared with very few people. All that happened was the production of SL-53, but only some eighteen months later, and to limited effect (as Chapter 12 demonstrated). A recognition of the need for training was there, but none was implemented before Clapham. And, of course, a Regional Testing Team was established under Mr Bailey, who was saddled with a huge workload, insufficient staff, no management direction and not enough emphasis on the importance of, and the implications behind, his team's origins. Indeed, 'No attempts were made by the Testing Team to develop training courses in their first year of operation'. In August 1987, in completing Bailey's annual performance appraisal, Davies did note that 'Bailey should spend more time on this aspect of his work'. But between August and Christmas 1987, Bailey only managed to produce a single page of handwriting, a draft entitled *Functional Testing*, 'listing a number of topics that such a course should cover'. As Hidden wrote, this reflected 'both an overall misconception as to the requirements of proper testing and at the same time the "prestige" that was attached to functional testing while other testing aspects were relegated to lower positions.'

If all that wasn't enough, a similar wrong-side failure occurred at Queenstown Road – the next station after Clapham Junction on the line into Waterloo – on 14 June 1988. Again, a signal had cleared directly from red to green instead of red to yellow, thus giving a false sense of the distance between one train and another. In this case, the wrong-side failure occurred on a straight stretch of track, so the driver anticipating the yellow could see the train ahead and could thus detect that the signal was wrong to clear to green. But, again, there had been a design error (a drawing being issued which omitted a track circuit from the signal's controls). And again, the error had not been picked up by the Design Office, nor during the testing of the signal on the ground. The difference this time was that the incident had been investigated by Bailey himself. It was he who identified the errors, he who made a report, but he too who failed to consider how the lessons could be conveyed to the workforce, and what lessons there were for the management. That said, he did realise that 'a lack of continuity among the checking staff' was in the causal chain, recognised this was unavoidable in a project like WARS and saw that 'managerial control need[ed] tightening in this respect'. He also expressed his concern that the hapless tester had lacked preparation, experience and expertise, but did not ask how those above him could have allowed this to happen. As those above him 'seemed satisfied by the taking of disciplinary proceedings against the supervisor concerned', this is hardly surprising.

Bailey made his report to John Deane, Area Signal Engineer (Works) at Wimbledon, who in turn made a report to Roger Penny, Area S&T Engineer (South West). Deane said the tester 'must bear the brunt of the incident due to his sloppy methods'. Deane also wrote of the need to avoid recurrences, as 'with the pressures and tightness of the WARS programme, coupled with a mixed bag of site staff, our integrity will again be challenged'.

The cynic might query the use of the word 'integrity', though the cynic might also spot the links in the causal chain joining up with worrying regularity. Not that *all* the links were in place just yet.

Chapter 15

A & O III

When you reorganise, you bleed.
Cited in Gerard Fiennes, *I Tried to Run a Railway*, 1967

Back at the start of May 1988, before the spectre of Clapham darkened their front pages, the papers were full of the killing of three RAF servicemen in the Netherlands, the proposed Poll Tax, the withdrawal of Soviet troops from Afghanistan and the re-election of François Mitterrand as President of France. The minds of most working on S&T equipment on the Southern, however, were filled with an initiative known as Administration and Organisation III, better known in conversation as 'A&O III'.

We have met A&O III in previous chapters, but now it has a name. It was a wide-reaching plan, designed to cut admin costs, bring more delegation to a new Area Management tier and 'ensure a strong contractual relationship' between that tier (on the operations side) and the sub-sector level of BR. Sectorisation had come a long way since 1982, the original sectors having spawned subordinate offspring, those on the freight side involving the different commodities carried (petroleum, aggregates, etc), those on the passenger side focussing largely on lines of route or operating area. As we have seen, most of the subsidiary businesses had also been sold off and the focus had moved towards a situation in which one part of BR would in effect bill another for services rendered. With this in mind, A&O III would help contracts to be drawn up 'with the person on the production side who was personally responsible for the delivery of that service to the business side at the standard required'. Not that A&O III was all about S&T, nor even all about the Southern. Peter Rayner, then Regional Operations Manager for the London Midland Region, would later write of it in the context of the 'same old pressures for more staff to be cut'. For him, it meant hacking away at 'the very back-up which gave [BR] quality: spare drivers, extra relief staff, extra carriage cleaners'.[69] It was also a distraction, on both a personal and professional level.

Consider Clifford Hale. Hale, the Regional S&T Engineer who'd insisted instructions be followed, who'd failed to brief Bailey on Oxted, had nevertheless suffered S&T Department reorganisations in 1982, 1984 and 1986. Now it was happening again. Anyone who's worked through a world being reorganised will recognise the sensation of the carpet moving beneath one's feet, of the lack of control, of being a pawn in someone else's game. When A&O III was first put forward in early 1987, Hale was worried that such a wide-ranging reorganisation would lead to bleeding, would need more staff and would therefore fall at the first hurdle. He was also worried that splitting 'regional' functions into 'area' ones might deplete their effectiveness, citing Bailey's three-man Regional Testing Team as an example. This had only been set up in August 1986 but would be disbanded and replaced by one tester in each of the Region's three areas (South Western, South Central and South Eastern).

As much delegation was involved with the proposed structure, Hale would also lose control of the project engineers, a bad move for him as it was through them that he 'exercised [the] responsibility for investment schemes and expenditure'. He decided to produce an alternative set of proposals. In this he had the support of Southern Region General Manager Gordon Pettitt. His thinking took him to something he called his '"matrix" solution', which left the management at each depot untouched and created three 'area business liaison engineers', who would report directly to him. This would minimise the change to local management, supervisors and technicians, but not affect the changes seen as needed at senior management level. It would also keep the Regional Testing Team intact.

At first, the proposals seemed to find favour with other managers in and around the Pettitt sphere. Alas, Network SouthEast Director Chris Green was not among them. In the world of sectorisation, the sector held sway and Green felt Hale's matrix would not strengthen the relationship between business manager and engineer, felt indeed that it 'missed the whole principle of delegation'. The Southern should 'fall into line with the other three regions which had a contractual relationship to provide services to Network SouthEast'. Hale was told to drop his idea, but did win a point inasmuch as, at a meeting on 22 December 1987, Pettitt, David Rayner (Joint Managing Director Railways) and Ken Hodgson (Director Signals & Telecommunications) agreed that extra staff would be needed to implement A&O III in full.

What followed was like a Cabinet reshuffle, a football transfer or any number of other metaphors you may wish to consider. Hidden called the arrangements 'cumbersome', but they had been agreed between the management and the unions, so everyone got a letter telling them they were being made redundant from the existing organisation. They then had to apply for posts within the new one, about which the only information was a short sentence, and for which no interviews were held. Many were not successful in their first application. Like Dray. Many 'experienced a change in the geographical location of their post and for a substantial number this was some distance from their homes with resultant personal difficulties'. Like Dray.

But not everyone suffered; while there was the uncertainty that came with re-application, for members of staff like Hemingway and Bumstead, what they had been doing at South Lambeth they simply went on to do at Wimbledon, though Bumstead was reportedly less happy with the staff brought in from other depots, as he was unaware of what they could do and how well they could do it. He also didn't care for some of his supervisor colleagues or for the chain of command. What in fact happened was the more junior you were, the less affected you were (although many managers were inexperienced and those more senior now had dramatically different roles).

As Hidden noted, 'poor working practices, unsatisfactory training and incomplete testing had all existed before the reorganisation'. The reorganisation did not cause it, but failed to 'come to grips' with it. Hence, S&T Supervisor Jim Lippett noticed poor levels of workmanship, but did not want to 'rock the boat', as he was 'an outsider in charge of a workforce that had worked closely together for a number of years'. He also had to go through Bumstead, 'who was suffering from low morale because of all the newcomers'. Furthermore, while it was Dray who omitted the wire count, Chapter 13 showed that Callander would have done exactly the same thing had he remained in his pre–May 1988 post. As Hidden put it more eloquently, 'the new brooms swept as little and as ineffectively as the old'.

And yet the question remained as to exactly why all this reorganisation had been so necessary anyway.

Chapter 16

Cap in Hand

In politics, there is no use looking beyond the next fortnight.
Joseph Chamberlain, 1886

When Paul Channon announced that a public inquiry into Clapham was to be set in motion, some of the questions put to him in the House earned the disapprobation of journalist and 'political sketchwriter' Matthew Parris. Some, whether intentionally or not however, hit something like a nail on something like its head. One such came from Robert Adley, Conservative Member for Christchurch, who called for 'a list of how many signal and track improvement schemes [were being] delayed pending the availability of funds under the public service obligation grant'.[70] Adley – a railway enthusiast and author himself – was right of course: funding, and the allocation of it, had been key to the whole Waterloo Area Resignalling Scheme.

By the late Seventies, the condition of the Walker-era installation had deteriorated such that concerns had started to be raised about reliability. As a result, in 1978, the Southern Region's General Manager put forward a Project Development Paper on 'the essential renewal of signalling equipment', as BR was then doing, or planning to do, in and around London Bridge and London Victoria. At this stage, the Waterloo plan envisaged work beginning early in 1982 and being completed by November 1986. Any later would have meant a substantial amount of work just to keep the system going, but all 1982 brought was authority to renew the interlocking at Waterloo station.[71] Work on the full WARS project did not begin in 1983, or 1984 either. Hidden wrote that 'the Court did not inquire' into its early years 'and therefore sought no evidence upon which it would be possible to make a finding as to whether or not [the project] was deferred because it had to compete for limited funds until the safety situation was so grave that the investment had to be authorised'. There is enough implication in these words to suggest that Adley was on to something.

The short answer is that he was; the short answer involves the post–Serpell need to cut costs, whose containment within the signalling world was 'rather limited' during most of the decade, despite the introduction of cost-reducing technologies like Solid State Interlocking (SSI), first used at Leamington Spa in 1985, and RETB equipment, which had come to the Dingwall-Kyle line in 1984, and would be extended to the Inverness-Wick/Thurso, East Suffolk, West Highland, and Cambrian lines by 1989.

The long answer, though, is rather longer, and has a timespan that's longer still.

Competition Element

Chapter 4 clarified that the future tends to come more slowly than many of us think. Often, though, this is less about the idea itself than the availability of money to make it work. As you might expect, the government had started to exercise tighter controls over the railways' parlous finances after nationalisation in 1948, but one could argue that government policy had been responsible for getting them to that state in the first place (Chapter 5). Indeed, the industry's route to serious loss-making really began when a previous government sold off a large number of army surplus lorries after the Great War. This allowed private hauliers to proliferate and undercut the railway. When coupled with improving vehicle technology and road surfaces, this burgeoning industry – and its bus-based equivalent – began to grow.

When nationalisation was being mooted around this time, and there was talk of introducing a new transport ministry, many feared that rail would dominate to the detriment of road. According to authors David Brandon and Martin Upham, a 'pro-road group of MPs' emerged, 'who campaigned vigorously against both the nationalisation proposal and the likelihood of the ministry being in thrall to the railway lobby'.[72] In the event, the railways were not nationalised and the Ministry of Transport turned out to have a road transport bias when it was created in 1919. When nationalisation *did* come – under Clement Attlee's Labour Administration – many of the Big Four's shareholders received generous payments, which – continue Brandon and Upham – 'created a millstone around the neck of the railways until most of the debt was written off in the 1960s'. In the Conservative Party, furthermore, 'there were influential people who had been directors of the Big Four or major shareholders and they never missed an opportunity to deride and debunk every aspect of the nationalised railways'. They found it 'expedient to forget the extent of this debt burden', while encouraging governments to aid the expansion of road haulage and private motoring.

Nationalisation had created a British Transport Commission, which the Labour government established to provide 'an efficient, adequate, economical and properly integrated system of public inland transport and port facilities within Great Britain for passengers and goods'. The railways – overused and under-maintained as they battled to get troops, military equipment and evacuees to the right place at the right time, and then under-compensated and under-renewed when the job had been done – would soon be competing with a road haulage industry freed from the shackles of such integration by the Transport Act of 1953.

This later legislation was brought in by the Conservative government of 1951 and saw a further 20,000 lorries sold off to private firms, which – like their earlier counterparts – could (and would) undercut the railway, something that increasing numbers of freight customers went on to exploit, particularly after a strike over pay and conditions called by the Associated Society of Locomotive Engineers and Firemen (ASLEF), from midnight on 28 May 1955. The first major railway stoppage for thirty years, it lasted seventeen days, but cost the railway £12 million in lost revenue, and saw some with consignments to send switch to road. Many did not come back when the men went back to work.

Of course, the railway had not helped itself by its apparent profligacy when it tried to modernise. Its Modernisation Plan had been supported by the government, which loaned some £1,200 million of public money to be spent over fifteen years on mechanisation, more colour-light signalling, more permanent way improvements, and the substitution of steam by diesel and electric traction. The trouble was, financial pressures, coupled with a belief that getting rid of steam was the answer, led to too many different locomotive types being ordered too quickly. Many did not work well and never would. Add in the building of new marshalling yards at a time when wagonload freight traffic was dwindling and it must have seemed that money was draining away like water from a broken bath – an apt simile, as Whitehall saw the railways following it down the plughole.

At the same time, a rise in disposable income meant that more people could afford a car: in 1951, there were 2.1 million of them on Britain's roads; in 1954, there were 2.7 million; by 1960, there would be 4.9 million. If nothing else, it made sense for politicians 'to court the approval of motorists', who made up 'an increasingly large part of the electorate'.

In light of all this, and despite the fact that passenger receipts had risen by £2 million and operating costs had fallen in 1959, in 1960

Prime Minister (and former GWR director) Harold Macmillan told the Commons that 'the railway system must be remodelled to meet current needs, and the Modernisation Plan must be adapted to this new shape'.[73] His Transport Minister, Ernest Marples, decreed that the Ministry would scrutinise all projects in excess of £250,000.

Marples requires some digression here. As co-owner of the Marples Ridgway construction company, he had been involved in the building of motorways. To avoid any conflict of interest when he became Transport Minister, he is believed to have divested himself of his shares to his wife. He had resigned as Managing Director on entering Parliament, but retained 80 per cent of his holding, continued to attend the company AGM and continued to meet Ridgway for lunch, but – for as long as he was a minister – received no dividends, director's fees, salary or other sums apart from expenses incurred on the company's behalf. When he moved from Postmaster General to the Ministry of Transport, however, it was made clear that he needed to 'explain and justify' his interest to the Commons. This he did, recounting his resignation and how he 'immediately' took steps to sell his shares when he became Minister of Transport. 'I think I should tell the House,' he added, 'that the prospective purchasers have required me to undertake to buy the shares back from them at the price they are to pay if they ask me to do so after I have ceased to hold office. I myself have no option to buy the shares back.' Writing in *The Times* in 1972, however, David Jones and Andrew Lumsden noted that 'it might be said that if a minister keeps any chance of regaining his shareholding once he has left office, other than through purchases on the stock exchange, he retains throughout office a prospective interest in the good fortunes of the firm'. And yet the charge that Marples beat down the railways for his own private gain will not do, for – as

Brandon and Upham reiterate – the swell of pro-road, pro-personal transport opinion had been building for decades.

It was against this backdrop that he appointed the chairman of Tube Investments, Sir Ivan Stedeford, to find ways of reducing the Modernisation Plan's expense.[74] Before the Second World War, most government financial interference had involved controlling rates and fares. During the war, when the railways had been sequestrated for the war effort, attention started to turn to capital expenditure as well. So much power was therefore taken by those who had little or no knowledge of the complexities of railways, and little or no time to acquire it. Yet the sort of intense scrutiny practised by Stedeford's Special Advisory Group would never let up and pointed the way not only to Serpell (himself a former 'Stedeford' member), but also delays to projects like WARS. At the time, while Whitehall probably had a point, it could be argued that the railway's financial problems were way more complicated, coming not just from the spending, but also the strike, the growth in motor vehicle ownership and the growth in domestic airlines, which all combined to help turn a surplus into a loss and keep it there – so much so that even the most famous former Stedeford member, Dr Richard Beeching, could not put the railways 'in the black' again.

What was needed was a change of philosophy, and this seemed to come with the 1968 Transport Act. Brought to parliament by Barbara Castle, one of the few Transport Ministers to appreciate that railways had a social role to play in society, it came into force under her Labour colleague and successor Richard Marsh, who went on to become the chairman of BR in 1971. It was the fourth major piece of legislation since the war and the first to draw a distinction between BR's commercial business and its socially desirable (but unprofitable) side, Part IV outlining, for example, the availability of grants for unremunerative passenger services, where 'it is desirable for social or economic reasons that railway passenger services to and from the place or places in question should for the time being continue to be provided'.[75]

The 1968 Act not only wiped out BR's debt of £153 million, but also established Passenger Transport Executives (PTEs) in and around Greater Manchester, Glasgow, Merseyside, Tyneside and the West Midlands. The idea was that the PTEs would co-ordinate local bus and rail services, 'purchasing' the latter from BR on a contract basis. Grants were also available for the 'social' railway, including £400,000 for Paddington–Oxford services, £2.5 million for Glasgow North and South suburban services and £9 million for Southern Region commuter traffic.

The trouble was that working out the grants for individual routes proved to be extremely difficult. Salvation came from the European Economic Community, specifically Regulation 1191/69, which defined the 'public service obligation' (PSO) to which Adley had referred and which provided that '[f]inancial burdens devolving on transport undertakings by reason of the maintenance of [their] obligations … be subject to compensation made in accordance with common procedure laid down in this regulation'. The PSO 'was global, unallocated and paid as compensation to transport undertakings obliged to maintain "the provision of adequate transport services"'. It was adopted in the Railways Act 1974, which also cut BR's capital debt from £438.7 million to £250 million and offered financial aid to businesses setting up private freight sidings.

If that sounds too good to be long-lived, it was. But railways do not exist in a vacuum, and their history is not some protracted boxing match with a railway servant in one corner and a government official in the other, each slugging it out in the name of cuts or continuity. There is another world beyond the boundary fence, and it always plays a part.

Rising Inflation

Like the WARS project, the APT faced the slings and arrows of the economy. In *APT: The Untold Story* (2016), David N. Clough records that the train's development had been 'hamstrung by resource constraints arising from the state of BR's finances during the economic downturn in the early 1980s', although the APT project was having problems long before that.

In 1973, the USA's support of Israel during that year's Arab-Israeli war led the Organization of Petroleum Exporting Countries (OPEC) to impose an oil embargo that led in turn to fuel shortages and widespread price rises. It sent inflation into the stratosphere and helped keep it there. It also spelled the end for the experimental (but thirsty) gas turbine–powered version of the APT, although – ironically – the Scottish Region saw traffic increases around this time, with construction materials being transported for the construction of a dry dock at Nigg, near Invergordon, for the British National Oil Corporation's North Sea oil fields.

By the scorching summer of 1976, Britain's annual rate of inflation had risen to 26 per cent. The value of the pound had also dropped from $2.00 at the start of the year to $1.70. The economy was in crisis and the only way out seemed to be to borrow. In June, the Labour Government had borrowed around £3 billion from the central banks of Canada, France, Germany, Japan, Switzerland and the United States, but it was not going to be enough. As Prime Minister James Callaghan explained at his party conference in Blackpool that autumn, the country needed to 'get back to fundamentals', by making 'labour costs at least comparable with those of our major competitors', by 'improving the productivity of both labour and capital' and by not printing '"confetti money" to pay ourselves more than we produce'.

Though hugely unpopular with many in the Cabinet, another loan was sought from the International Monetary Fund (IMF) – for $3.9 billion, the largest in the fund's history. With it came the condition that major cuts be made to public spending. For the wider public sector, there had long been a bid to curb wages and keep them in line with inflation. This was the 'social contract', in which government and unions agreed modest pay rises that would not inflame the rate of inflation. The IMF negotiations helped galvanise that policy, as it was based on the Treasury's forecast that the Public Sector Borrowing Requirement (PBSR) for 1977/78 would be £10.5 billion. For BR specifically, it would see the PSO fall, such that – if freight grants are taken into account too – the level of support in 1979 would end up being 20 per cent lower than that for 1975. But as we saw in Chapter 5, the government's controls on public spending beyond BR led to a series of public sector strikes, whose unions' challenge to the 'social contract' led to a general election. The irony is that the Treasury's figures had been wrong; the PBSR for 1977/78 turned out to be just £5.6 billion. In the end, only half the IMF loan needed to be drawn; the irony further is that it had been paid off by 2 January 1979, just a few months before the 3 May election, which Labour lost and saw the Conservatives (under Margaret Thatcher) take power. Despite this, a recession still came, and – again as we saw in Chapter 5 – this is where sectorisation essentially came in.

Sectorisation had made Sector Managers responsible for the financial performance of their sector, a move which prompted fears that safety expenditure desired by BR's operational side might be deferred by its commercial side, the latter – as with all nationalised industries – being required to show a positive return on its government-set capital investment programmes. In time, this financial responsibility would lead to initiatives like A&O III. In time, it would lead Maurice

Holmes, BR's Director of Operations, to voice his concerns that 'past high safety standards [were] starting to be eroded by a change in the railway culture'. 'I would not like,' he added, 'a major disaster with loss of life to be the reason that forced British Rail to invest in modern safety aids'. In 1982, though, the sector linked to WARS was London & South East, which was arguably still reeling from an examination by the Monopolies and Mergers Commission two years before, which had looked at the efficiency of commuter services in its catchment area.[76] At this stage, it had yet to morph into the red, white and blue world of Chris Green, yet even to launch its successful 'Gatwick Express' services. In fact, it made a loss of £310 million in 1982, and while this would drop to £248 million in 1983, it would worsen again before it improved.

The rest of the country wasn't in a much better state; by 1982, production had plummeted, while inflation and unemployment had soared, three million being out of work at the start of the year. Employment Secretary Norman Tebbit had won few friends when he told the 1981 Conservative Party Conference how his father had 'got on his bike and looked for work' in the bleak 1930s, but it was Thatcher's refusal at the previous year's event to 'turn' on the tax cuts made in the June 1979 budget, and her chancellor's pledge in that budget to 'roll back the boundaries of the public sector', that would have further-reaching consequences for BR.

The drivers of inflation in 1979 were high oil prices brought about this time by a real (and perceived) drop in oil output in the wake of a revolution in Iran, coupled with a high "confetti-covered" public sector wage bill. Little could be done about the former and trying to control the latter, as the new government knew, had led to the fall of the old government. Putting up taxes could help, but the humiliation it would cause and damage it would do to business meant it was not really an option for Thatcher's administration. Controlling public spending and public sector borrowing it therefore had to be. There would be an attempt in 1981, the Budget that March winding the PSBR back towards £10 million. It seemed to work – the following day saw interest rates fall from 14 to 12 per cent. But, as historian Graham Stewart later wrote, it was just a 'mirage', a run on the pound that October seeing interest rates ramp back up to 16 per cent. It was in this climate that, Thatcher aside, the U-turn came regarding BR's subsidiary businesses, in which BR had hoped to sell shares to raise funds and help them flourish.

The need to cut public sector funding would also have an effect on WARS, of course. Big projects like this needed *investment* capital. Recession and the rising cost of the Falklands War had stymied many schemes, but mindful of a barely adequate investment ceiling of around £400 million per annum, and mindful no doubt of the 'increasingly tight constraints' being placed on the government-set 'External Financing Limit' – the amount BR was permitted to obtain from outside BR, from government subsidy, level crossing grants, loans, the capital value of assets leased, and so on – the Board blocked all major new investment in 1982.

In October 1983, the newly re-elected government's new Secretary of State for Transport, Nicholas Ridley, instructed BR to reduce the PSO to £635 million by 1986, rather than 1988 as BR had suggested in its own corporate plan. Ridley wrote that 'the guiding objective should be to run an efficient railway, providing good value for money', with 'reliable, attractive and punctual' services 'at acceptable fares and charges'. This and the PSO cut were to be achieved 'without a major programme of rail closures'.

As we saw in Chapter 6, it was fortunate that Reid got on so well with Ridley, and that Thatcher trusted Ridley, but though this would allow more money to be made available for investment, there were plenty of hoops for the organisation to jump through *en route*.

The first was BR's own Investment Committee, from which approval for any project costing over £1 million had to be sought. Anything over £5 million also had to be submitted to the Department of Transport, which categorised projects at this level into those about which Ridley needed to be informed, those for which he needed to see the appraisal and submission details, and those requiring his authorisation. And of course approval would only come if the project kept within the External Financing Limit.

In May 1983, BR had been told by the Department that WARS – though since discussed, deferred and 'reduced in cost and scope' – would be called in for approval. Had they been quicker off the mark, this would have been from Ridley's predecessor Tom King, but WARS continued to be discussed internally before a detailed submission was made to the Investment Committee in September 1984. The scheme was expected to cost £32.5 million and would rationalise and resignal the Waterloo area, which would then be controlled by a new box at Wimbledon, thereby allowing thirteen older boxes to be closed and 74 posts to be cut, saving some £737,000 a year. It would also cut down the expensive maintenance outlay required to keep the old system in operation.

Unfortunately, the signal failure rate had risen by a worrying 26 per cent, meaning that 'the integrity of the signalling system [was now] at risk'. Worse still, there had been 'three "wrong-side" failures due to the condition of the equipment', one of which involved a signal failing to show a red aspect because a technician touched a wire during routine maintenance and it broke through 'brittleness caused by age'. 'To permit further deterioration,' the submission went on, 'is completely unacceptable'. It is interesting to reflect here on what Serpell had to say on signalling renewals:

> It is not easy to assess when signalling renewals will be required, [but] the Board say that this requires an engineering judgement which anticipates operational failure of the equipment. As the equipment is designed to 'fail safe', we consider that *this engineering judgement may have been applied rather conservatively. In principle, older mechanical equipment should be replaced by its modern counterpart only when the rise in its maintenance costs results in uneconomic overall costs.*' (author's italics).[77]

Over the six years that the project had squirmed at the whim of the economy and such economics, there was nothing 'conservative' now about the need to implement WARS. In fact the work had moved from being merely necessary to absolutely vital.

The Serpell report was right about railway equipment being designed to fail to a safe condition, however. It was a lesson hard won over a long history and explained why (for example) the white signal lights used to denote a 'clear' run were later changed to the more familiar green, lest a broken red lens fooled drivers into thinking they had an unhindered run. A wrong-side failure would create such a misapprehension, so was therefore highly dangerous and to be avoided.

Thankfully, on 1 October 1984, the Investment Committee endorsed the submission, which then went to Ridley for authorisation. He had already authorised the electrification of the East Coast Main Line that July on the understanding that journey times would be cut and productivity would be improved. Reid called it 'the most important investment decision … in over 25 years'. Authorisation for WARS came on 19 December. By this time, the recession had passed, and revenues from North Sea oil – discovered in 1969, piped ashore from 1975, a net export from 1983 – were bringing in £12 billion in tax; the British National Oil Corporation had also been sold for £500 million the previous year.

It was about money; it was about oil, and the British oil poured on the troubled waters of the British economy helped pay the benefits of the three million unemployed, helped cut taxes, helped balance the budget, and arguably helped to allow the planning work on WARS to begin.

Chapter 17

Best Laid Plans

Nothing in progression can rest on its original plan.

Edmund Burke,
Letter to the Sheriffs of Bristol, 1777

The Clapham accident was all about failings; failings in the installation of WARS, failings in the management of staff, failings on the ladder up to government level. As Hidden would record, one major 'rung' involved the planning of the project, which began once the green light had at last been given. On 13 February 1985, a meeting was convened to decide – among other things – whether to bring the works into operation in stages ('stageworks') or to condense changeovers into 'major commissionings'. For track circuits, a 'rolling programme of conversions' was preferred, but it was decided that there was no need to commission the signals themselves in advance, as leaving them would allow the old ones to stand sentinel for as long as possible. This would avoid the need for periods where the railway was totally blocked, the requisite re-routings, workarounds and contingency plans for keeping trains moving being much harder to implement on a busy commuter network in the week, after all.

It was a good plan, a sensible plan, a workable plan too. As Roy Bell, BR Signal Engineer, said when he presented his expert evidence, leaving the signals until the 'commissioning weekend' would have ensured the minimum disturbance of the old system, which would also have meant less work on the circuitry in the relay room. But then it all changed.

Two years later, on 11 February 1987, a meeting at South Lambeth was held to enable the S&T Department to present details of its programme to meet the agreed main commissioning dates. It was not going to be easy. 'The time scale for the scheme allows a little "fall-back" time for Stages 3 to 6,' the minutes record, 'but none for Stages 7 and 8.' Commissioning work on the former was due to begin on 2 and 3 July 1988, and from then until the commissioning of Stage 8B in August 1989, there would be no spare weekends. The times shown on the proposed programme were those 'required to complete the work'. Reduction in these times therefore increased the risk of the project overrunning.

Attached to the minutes were proposals that had been drawn up by Callander, while serving as the Senior Construction Assistant at South Lambeth. He had put them together towards the end of 1986. They set out the work for the whole period, including the weekend of 26 and 27 November 1988. When Callander produced his plan, Stages 1 (Waterloo) and 2 (Vauxhall and Raynes Park) had already been completed, but 3 to 9 remained. To make sure the deadline could be achieved, he divided the work into practical sections. His plan was devised over a year after the February 1985 meeting, at which he had not been present, but whose spirit he managed to reflect in all but one element. The key difference was that Callander felt the new signals should be brought into use gradually. He thought this would *reduce* disruption to traffic and thought it would negate temporary differences in the 'overlap' (a safety margin proven by track circuits to be clear of other trains).

Callander also worked out the total number of conversions that had to be completed and looked at the number of weekends available. After consulting with colleagues, he decided that an average of nine track circuits could be converted from old to new in one shift. When he worked this fact up into a timetable of his own, it became clear that there were indeed very few spare weekends, that there was very little room for slippage and that seven-day working would be necessary. As a result, he requested three more months between Stages 6 (New Malden/Berrylands) and 7 (Clapham Junction) and three more between Stages 7 and 8 (Wimbledon).

Callander's plan went unapproved and unheeded. Had it 'been put into operation correctly the system would have been safe,' wrote Hidden. Maybe. Maybe not, for if it *had* been approved, it would have remained stuck in 1986 as far as staffing levels were concerned. The trouble was that the staffing levels themselves did not. In the two years between 1986 and 1988, BR lost a lot of skilled people, people attracted by the burgeoning electrical communications industry, companies like British Telecom and Mercury being able to offer higher rates of pay and more 'social' hours than the railway. Why work all the overtime you can, all the weekends you can, for the good of your family if you never get to spend any time *with* your family? Why bother trying to acquire a video player if you're never at home to watch a film, or the latest electronic gizmos for Christmas if you fall asleep while the children are unwrapping them? People were starting to want more, and they did not feel they should be running themselves into the ground to get it. As ASLEF's Assistant General Secretary Derrick Fullick told the BBC, there was a 'big shortage of rail staff in the whole of the south-east, due to the poor wages. [...] Doesn't matter what grade you are, the wages are bloody lousy.'[78]

The older members of staff retained something of the old culture of allegiance to the railway, the culture in which railways got into the blood, which instilled pride, respected skill – the culture in which railways were more than just a job yet were a 'job for life'. The dichotomy was neatly illustrated with Hidden's example of the 'technician who … joined another industry, but … returned to BR,' but whose son 'made the same move' and never went back.

BR was no longer in a position to be able to resolve 'recruitment and retention problems' by relying on the goodwill, enthusiasm and loyalty of men who were happy to see a job through (and happy to double their incomes). The trouble was that BR was unaware of the fact. Indeed, it was only after the May 1988 reorganisation, when questioned on the timescale by Penny, that Deane and Callander explained that the programme remained 'tight but achievable', as long as no more senior technicians left. At best, as Hidden noted, it was 'not a carefully thought out view and was not checked against the timetable'. At worst, it was practically an oxymoron. Either way, it meant the already tight timetable got even tighter, and meant the opportunities – and also the need – for overtime increased enormously.

'This lack of planning and mismanagement of the workload,' wrote Hidden, 'was a wholly ineffective use of resources, both human and financial.' Furthermore, the most important, safety-critical elements of the work were always carried out at weekends. Saturdays and Sundays should therefore have been *particularly* well planned, to make sure adequate numbers of suitably qualified staff were available, aware of their responsibilities, and not jaded by constant seven-day working week after week. It was certainly 'not a safe working practice to allow so many men to work excessive levels of overtime for a sustained period'. The work should also have been organised to make sure supervisors were fulfilling their proper role and not acting as senior technicians (as of course Bumstead would do when he should have been supervising Hemingway).

At the hearing, the Joint Managing Director (Railways), David Rayner, explained that, if a job was insufficiently staffed, that job would be postponed. One can imagine the sectors being less than welcoming to any delay to a programme on which their timetables had been planned. Instead, there was a prevailing (and frankly probably accurate) belief that the timeframe was 'set in stone' – and no one wanted to suggest any target could not be met.

Part of the problem here was a lack of control. We have already seen this in relation to BR's financial situation, but there were also issues with the control of the design, BR's own installation, and the work done by contractors. 'In many organisations,' Hidden added, 'the title "Project Manager" would cover responsibility for all four aspects.' For WARS, financial control was carried out by a *so-called* Project Manager, who in reality was a member of the General Manager's staff outside the S&T Department. His job was to make sure the scheme was keeping to budget. Below the Regional S&T Engineer, responsibility for the actual work was somewhat scattered. The designing was done within the Region's Drawing Office, which prior to May 1988 reported to the Regional S&T Engineer. Control of BR's installation work and day-to-day management was carried out by the local depot managers, who reported to the Signal Works Engineer. The contractors were organised under a separate 'Project Engineer'. Thus, 'below the Regional S&T Engineer *no one person* was responsible for all aspects of project management' (my italics). After May 1988, the situation was complicated further when Design Office work and project control became the responsibility of the Director of S&T, Ken Hodgson, but with the same staff at the same place (that is, Southern House in Croydon).

'In an ideal situation,' Hidden went on, 'there should be a strong "Project Engineer/Manager" responsible directly for all four aspects of the project. If these cannot all come within his chain of command then they should be established in a contractual relationship with those who will provide those other functions, without diminishing the Project Engineer/Manager's role or responsibility'. 'If this had been the situation on the WARS scheme,' he argued, 'one person could have reviewed the overall plan of works to make sure it met with strategic decisions already taken.' This person could have made sure that deadlines were both realistic and regularly reviewed and could have considered and reduced the competing claims of the drawing office, which was under pressure, lacked the time to produce modified drawings, lacked too the time to produce the accurate drawings required by installation staff.

In the years ahead, the rail industry, indeed all industries, would almost fetishize the cult of project management, so much so that it would – in some places – merely add bureaucracy where it was not needed, and put people who knew little in charge of those who know much. And yet there is nothing new under the sun; professional rail staff resented the edicts of their civil servant masters during the Second World War. As Michael Bonavia described it in *The Four Great Railways* (1980), 'Despite the wholehearted way in which the railways responded to all policy directives on important issues, there was an undercurrent of resentment from time to time among professional railwaymen at receiving instructions from those whom they considered amateurs.'

All that said, there can be no doubt that someone who stands tall and sees all aspects of a project will benefit those requesting, those producing and those receiving what that project will bring. But if that vision is true of projects, it is also true of the whole concept of safety…

Chapter 18

Eyes Everywhere?

Many are the things that man seeing must understand.
Not seeing, how shall he know what lies in the hand of time to come?

Sophocles,

Ajax, c.442 BC

In signalling, equipment is designed to revert to a safe condition if something goes wrong. Sometimes, though, as we have seen, there can be a wrong-side failure, which could lead to an unsafe condition and a false impression of reality. In railways more generally, as we have also seen, there can be collisions with cattle, collisions at level crossings, bridge collapses … and signals passed at danger. And it was signals passed at danger that presented the greatest threat to safety in the minds of many. It was not hard to see why; Colwich in 1986, after all, had been particularly nasty, but then came Purley and Bellgrove, just as Hidden's inquiry was getting under way.

Purley occurred on 4 March 1989, when a passenger train struck another after it had crossed from the Up Slow line to the Up Fast. Five people were killed and 88 were injured. The accident at Bellgrove came two days later when a train struck an incoming service, killing the driver, killing a passenger, and injuring 53 more. Both lines had been fitted with BR's <u>Automatic Warning System</u> (AWS). AWS had been developed after nationalisation and rolled out from 1956 onwards. Still in use, it features a permanent magnet in the track, normally positioned

180 metres on the approach to a signal. The driver receives a 'bell' whenever the signal is green, and a 'horn' at any other aspect. If a restrictive aspect is encountered, the brakes are automatically applied unless the driver acknowledges the warning within the allowed time period; the black disc indicator in the cab then adjusts to show yellow sectors in a 'sunflower' pattern. At Purley, the driver had cancelled the warnings, but not heeded them; at Bellgrove, the driver started against a red at the end of the platform, having heeded the guard's dispatch signal over the signal aspect, whose AWS warning would have been cancelled prior to pulling in.

Bellgrove also resulted from the reconfiguration of the track layout in April 1987. In brief, a 'single lead junction' had been installed, in which two tracks go into one before the intersection with another line. This cut down on pointwork (and so, maintenance and cost), but could put trains on a collision course if a SPAD occurred. After investigating a similar accident (at Newton, on 21 July 1991), Peter Rayner, by then Director of Psychometric Testing at the BR Board, was moved to write a paper in which he 'tried to establish how it was possible for a decision to be made that created a track layout which would have been laughed at in the industry a few years earlier'. He put the responsibility on BR's 1982 edict to rationalise infrastructure, 'and its strict interpretation in Scotland by [the] Provincial [sector]'.[79] Eventually, BR carried out a study of all platform starting signals to assess the risk of collision should one be passed at danger. A number of measures were then recommended, dependent on risk level, from adding points ahead of the signal to derail an errant train at low speed ('trap points') to changing high-risk single lead junctions to double junctions. The Driver Reminder Appliance, a manual switch that gives a visual indication of the signal ahead and prevents the application of power, also came in at this point.[80]

Pilloried in the press, the driver of the train involved in the Purley accident – Robert Morgan – was sentenced to eighteen months in prison, but there was much more to the incident than human error. Take the signal Morgan had passed – T168, which had been installed in 1984. The investigation report noted that, while drivers had slightly longer to see it while in motion than the seven seconds considered acceptable for a 90-mph line, the sighting at T168 signal was 'poor', being obscured by the station buildings as trains approached. The investigation also noted that, while the signal in rear of T168, T178, had a sighting distance 'considerably better than the minimum requirement', it may have caused drivers to 'relax … concentration, not control the speed of the train properly and then find [themselves] surprised by the short sighting distance of [T168]'.

T168 had been passed at danger four times before the accident. One incident had involved a brake failure, but at least two of the other three had been 'Purleys in the making', SPADs in which the driver had continued past a danger signal despite having received prior AWS warnings. This and the sighting question were accepted by the court in 2007. The conviction was overturned, but sadly Morgan would live with his good name restored for just two more years. Though not expressed as causal to the accident at the time, the inferior sighting of T168 was acknowledged in the report's recommendation that a repeater signal (known as a 'banner repeater') be provided on the approach to Purley station to give an advance reminder of the signal's status to drivers.

In some ways, the 'Purley incidents' validated the fears that many Southern managers had always held about AWS.[81] There were essentially three reasons for the Region's apparent 'slowness' in this regard: first, installation was costly, given the close spacing of the Region's signals and the large number of multiple units that would have to be equipped; secondly, there was the technical difficulty of developing a reliable version for use on 'third rail' lines, where there was the possibility of false indications being given by stray earth currents; finally, and most importantly, there was a suspicion that AWS was not really suitable for the intensively worked, colour-light signalled sections in and out of the capital. The equipping of the lines from Woking to Waterloo showed that, when closely spaced four-aspect signals combined with close headway working, drivers were having to cancel warnings at cautionary signals in 'rapid succession'. Under these conditions, the warnings could lose their significance and cause a driver to cancel without thinking, perhaps even when approaching a red.[82] Purley, if not Bellgrove, suggested that they might have been right. (Much further forward, Ladbroke Grove would suggest much the same thing, as we shall see in Chapter 22.)

In a bid to overcome fears about repetitive cancellation, work had begun on what became known as SR AWS (Southern Region AWS, later renamed Signal Repeating AWS) far back in the late 1960s. This involved the in-cab indication of individual signal aspects and required the driver to acknowledge each indication by a separate and distinct action. It was based on work already being carried out by BR's Research Department at Derby and, if successful, could have been a first step towards fully automatic train operation. In the event, the project was plagued by technical difficulties and rising costs – to nearly three times that of the standard system.[83] When the Dartford and London Bridge re-signalling schemes were commissioned soon after, however, the Region found the new configuration allowed traffic to flow more freely, found too that drivers were facing 'a marked reduction in the number of consecutive restrictive signal aspects'.[84] A survey was carried out which showed the improvement to be sufficient for the Board to deem standard AWS sufficient for Southern conditions after all (albeit with stronger – 'green' – magnets to reach receivers mounted on the underframes of the Region's EMUs, as opposed to their bogies, as elsewhere on the network). The Southern began to install AWS at such a rate that, by the end of 1978, 436 of its route miles had been equipped. By the end of 1987, the national picture was such that 6,824 route miles (66 per cent of the total) were in a similar state.

SPADs were not a recent problem, and had been causal to many of the century's most high-profile accidents, including the multi-train collision at Harrow & Wealdstone, which killed 112 people on 8 October 1952, just as – in one of the bitter ironies of railway safety – AWS trials were beginning.[85] L.T.C. Rolt's literary litany of railway accidents, *Red for Danger*, discusses the accident as part of a long line of fatal SPAD events. As Hidden would later describe, 'the monitoring and investigation of SPADs' therefore 'received a great deal of attention', each incident requiring full reporting and 'thorough investigation' so that the 'appropriate learning' could be drawn out and taught. Purley and Bellgrove added two more to the count, which had been climbing such that, of the 843 SPADs in 1988, 87 had resulted in either derailment or collision. Monitoring these situations was clearly laudable and necessary. But what if, as in Clapham, a red signal actually showed green? This, for Hidden, was a key point.

Part of that problem was that 'wrong-side failure' was a '"catch-all" title which covered [a] whole spectrum of occurrences varying in gravity from the potentially disastrous to the least significant'. The latter could be an indicator light for a set of points, or a telephone at a level crossing; the former is what happened to WF138 signal on the morning of 12 December 1988. As Chapter 14 showed, incidents were starting to occur, and a pattern was starting to emerge, but wrong-side failures were (as Hidden put it) 'something of a poor relation' to SPADs and the right messages were not getting through to the right people.

Figures obtained for the hearing revealed there to have been 114 wrong-side failures in the WARS area between 1985 and 1988. Two involved work not checked correctly, two involved a signal showing a false aspect, one (at Waterloo on 19 November 1987) had occurred because a cable fault during installation led to points being wrongly set. There had also been fifteen wrong-side failures 'caused by inadequate testing' across the whole of the Southern between 1985 and 1987. Thirteen had been on the WARS project.

Reported failures were investigated by the Maintenance Department, but only those that led to an accident had to be reported to the Railway Inspectorate. Most of the time, there would be no accident and the report would be internal only. The trouble was that all-too-often the report would simply end with 'NFF', meaning 'no fault found'. After 'an alarming number' of signal failures in 1985, BR did introduce a new 'Fault Reporting and Maintenance Evaluation' computer system, known as FRAME, to aid reliability checking. Yet wrong-side failures were recorded therein as a single category. The fact that they were not split according to risk helped obscure the true picture. The devil was in the detail, but the detail just wasn't there.

Chapter 19

Where Responsibility Lies

When a man assumes a public trust, he should consider himself as public property.

Thomas Jefferson, to Baron von Humboldt,
Life of Jefferson, 1834

The devil was in the detail, yet Sir Robert Reid – the LNER man, the dependable man – assured the Court that the British Railways Board was committed to 'absolute safety', that no accident was acceptable. No one in fact would do anything other than put safety first.

Hidden respected Reid's sincerity but pointed out that the target had not been met, that the causes of Clapham 'were a combination of bad practice and mismanagement'. He agreed that there had been no 'deliberate decision to cut corners on safety', but felt the important issue was 'the priority accorded to [it]'. It was also clear to him that 'the bad working practices which were endemic in the S&T Department at the time of the accident [could not] have happened overnight'.

Hidden's Court was not a test of legal liability, but he was at pains to point out that the concluding chapter of his report would perforce be critical of some of those involved. Anything else would be 'an abdication of duty'. That said, before launching into all the attributed errors, he noted that 'almost without exception, those who gave … evidence … did so with conscientiousness, care, dignity and with a measure of frankness which was wholly to be admired' – especially as some of them left themselves wide open as a result. Furthermore, he knew there was 'almost no human action or decision that cannot be made to look more flawed and less sensible in the misleading light of hindsight'.[86]

In brief, the immediate cause of the Clapham accident was that the under-trained Hemingway made 'mistakes' on Sunday 27 November 1988. These were 'characteristic', stemming from 'poor working practices', and 'uncharacteristic', resulting both from interruption and from undertaking constant, repetitive work and excessive levels of overtime after probable poor nights of sleep, the like of which might be associated with an eight-month-old baby at home (a detail provided in the BR report, but not by Hidden).[87] Bumstead should have been supervising him more closely, but – perhaps to keep the job rolling, perhaps to get trains moving again – chose to work out on the track and failed to make a plan with Testing and Commissioning Engineer Dray about who would be doing what in preparation for the testing of the work done. Dray was somewhat disenfranchised by the whole May 1988 reorganisation anyway, but got little help from his immediate predecessor in the Testing and Commissioning role, the also-disenfranchised Callander, who did not follow procedures, new or otherwise, and whose handover to Dray was poor, leaving the latter unaware of his full testing duties. One thing Callander *did* do was try to work out a plan that would actually get WARS done on time. That plan went unheeded but was founded on outdated assumptions about staffing levels which were changing because staff expectations were changing along with its demographic.

Unaware of this was Jim Lippett, who – as Signal Works Assistant – was absent at weekends, had been reorganised into work with which he was unfamiliar, had 'turned his back on the bad working practices he saw and made no attempt to stamp them out'. Above Lippett, Geoff

Bailey – as Signal Works Engineer – was under-resourced, under-briefed by over-re-organised Regional S&T Engineer Clifford Hale and therefore did not carry out quality checks on the work in hand; he also failed to see the importance of undertaking wire counts and failed to share the lessons of the Queenstown Road wrong-side failure with those below or above. Above Bailey, John Deane – as Area Signal Engineer (Works) – and Roger Penny – as Area S&T Engineer – had been too inclined to blame the tester rather than the management when something went wrong.

Hidden also noted that 'there was no one individual responsible for [WARS] as a whole', that the planning of the work 'was not reviewed initially at a sufficiently senior level, nor … reviewed on a regular basis', that the day-to-day organisation was inefficient, and the timescale perceived as 'inflexible and … running very tight'. Furthermore, 'no-one had the power or the will to introduce more efficient arrangements [or] demand that the main commissioning dates be delayed'.

Reid had long since accepted responsibility on behalf of BR. It was the right thing to do. But if it was right, it was also wrong. Soon after Hidden presented his findings, James Reason, Professor of Psychology at the University of Manchester, published his theories on accident causation. It would later become known as the 'Swiss cheese model', in which a company's or industry's defence mechanisms against failure are modelled as a series of barriers, represented by slices of cheese. The holes in the slices signify weaknesses in parts of the system. When holes in each of the slices line up, it creates what Reason called a 'trajectory of opportunity', allowing a hazard to pass through and become a failure – or accident. The 'holes' in the Clapham case were clear; from front line error to supervision failure, management failure to (re-)organisational failure (and all the distraction and the short-term ineffectiveness of the new incumbents that goes with it), from a failure to learn to a failure to see that wrong-side failures were equally as important as SPADs. All these elements were ostensibly under the aegis of Reid and the Board, but Hidden also criticised the fact that it took six years to 'push' WARS through 'BR's investment authorisation machinery', and noted that the need for 'excessive amounts of overtime' to keep the project moving was down to there being 'too few staff' And the reason there were too few staff was 'BR's inability to recruit and keep sufficient workers'.

The reason BR could not recruit and keep sufficient workers was about conditions, but it was also about money. The reason why it took so long to get WARS through BR's own approval process, was the same reason it had 'sectorised' at the start of the decade – money. BR did not have much and the government wanted to give it less. And less. Clapham occurred in part, then, because BR did not have enough money to pay its staff wages comparable with the burgeoning electrical communications industry, was not permitted to make capital investment without government approval, and was under constant pressure to be 'more efficient' (which almost always translates as 'do more for less, and like it'). A shortcoming of Hidden's report is arguably that it was not explicit enough on this point, which of course reached across the whole of BR, not just one department in one Region.

Hidden wrote that 'the Court did not inquire' into the early years of WARS 'and therefore sought no evidence upon which it would be possible to make a finding as to whether or not [the project] was deferred because it had to compete for limited funds until the safety situation was so grave that the investment had to be authorised'. However, 'the possibility that such may have been the case [was] enough to make the point for the future'. Hidden recognised that 'the present investment constraints on BR are not as rigid as in the later seventies and early eighties [but] the progress of the WARS project [presented] a clear lesson to be learned for future investment projects with very significant safety benefits'.

It would be possible to make a political case out of this, turning it into an anti–Thatcher tirade. But the simple truth is that the truth is not nearly so simple. Economics are fickle, are subject to the slings and arrows of world events, like wars, like revolutions, like a simple desire for an improved standard of living. The chapter of knowledge is short, but the chapter of accidents is a very long one. So how far back does one look for the root of Clapham? After the wiring was installed in 1936, it began to deteriorate slowly, almost immediately, but expand that thought and Clapham would not have happened if the railways had not been invented. True, but hardly useful. When BR bought too many unproven diesel locomotives in the 1950s, however, it did incite greater scrutiny of its capital expenditure at a time when the cult of the private motor car was soaring. That scrutiny never ebbed – and perhaps with good reason.

It is fair to say that BR seemed to learn from the over-ordering of diesel locomotives, as the experience was not repeated when seeking a standard electric machine for the West Coast Main Line. A hundred locomotives were built, comprising five different types from five different manufacturers (including BR itself). The learning from this process was taken forward to the eventual standard type – the AL6, later Class 86. However, the learning may *not* have been carried forward to the 1970s. Clough makes the point that, in 1972, the Department of Transport expressed concern about the way the APT project was being managed. This concern would resurface and leads Clough to note that BR Board members and Department Heads in the mid-70s would probably have been around in more junior roles to witness the errors their (then) superiors had made with the Modernisation Plan. So 'surely,' he writes, 'this would have allowed them to appreciate that their counterparts in the DfT had equally long memories and did not want a similar debacle on their watch?'[88]

On top of this, when the Arab–Israeli war led to oil price rises in the early 1970s, it led the government to make cuts in public spending. The same happened with the Iranian Revolution of 1979. And when the Treasury got its figures wrong in 1976, it led to the acquisition of the largest IMF loan in history and yet more pressure on the nationalised BR. Not so much a set of Swiss cheese slices, more a full Emmental, with holes in every direction leading to an accident at the core.

Rewinding to the Commons on Tuesday 7 November 1989, we find Secretary of State for Transport Cecil Parkinson telling the assembly he was about to publish Hidden's findings. He reiterated everyone's 'deepest sympathy for the relatives and friends of the 35 people who died [and] the many people who were injured'. He remembered too 'the many others, both passengers and rescuers, who [bore] the mental scars of that harrowing day'.

Parkinson then summarised Hidden's findings, noting that the report had made 93 recommendations. 'Some,' he said, were 'directed towards preventing a recurrence of an accident of that type'; others were addressed to 'securing improvements in British Rail's management and organisational systems for safety'. Others were directed to the emergency services, and some were directed to the government. He asked BR 'to deal promptly with all the recommendations addressed to it, and to report to [him] on their implementation within three months'. He acknowledged that 'many of the recommendations [were] based on BR's suggestions or on the conclusions of BR's own internal inquiry', acknowledged too that BR had 'already taken action', although 'in some cases Sir Anthony Hidden recommend[ed] faster implementation'.

The Shadow Transport Secretary, John Prescott, felt the report exposed the way 'safety [had] suffered at the expense of financial and commercial considerations'. He asked if Parkinson agreed that the report revealed 'starkly the dangers of policies that led to the presence of overworked, exhausted staff, many of whom lacked proper training, and who suffered from low pay and poor morale'. For Prescott, this was down to 'a management that strove so hard to achieve tough financial and commercial targets set by the government that basic safety concerns were lost'. The report was thus 'a powerful indictment of both inadequate management and the government's policy'. Surely, he went on, 'the report demands a rethink by both the government and British Rail's senior management of the policies adopted over the past 10 years.'

Alas, Prescott tripped himself up by linking the drop in staff numbers on the S&T side to the '51 per cent cut ... in Government grants to British Rail over the same five-year period'. The debate thus descended into party politics. Parkinson refuted that 'safety had been put at risk because of shortage of funds'. Prescott, he said, had 'consistently [failed] to understand that British Rail's revenue ha[d] increased more quickly than the grant ... decreased'. Therefore, he went on, 'the cash resources available to British Rail for investment ha[d] been growing'. Indeed, British Rail was 'pursuing the biggest investment programme for 25 years'. Hidden apparently made it clear that 'even if there were constraints on investment expenditure in the late 1970s, when [Labour, Prescott's party] was in government, and the early 1980s, those constraints have been eased and that a full investment programme [was] now being carried through'. Parkinson chose not to mention the help his government had been given by the tax revenues from North Sea oil, and the sell-off of the British National Oil Corporation in 1982, both of which had been established under the Labour government of 1975.

The chapter of knowledge is short, but the chapter of accidents is long. The following day, the papers reported on the anger, bitterness and frustration of the relatives of the dead and injured. Christine

Clark, whose husband Glen had been killed, said Hidden had not gone far enough and called for BR to be 'prosecuted for negligence and incompetence'. Some wanted sackings, others wanted the lessons to be learned. Julian Dalrymple, who had lost his son, was understandably pessimistic. 'After a few months,' he told *The Times*, 'BR will forget all about it and go back to normal. Then there will be another tragedy.'

Clifford Hale did not forget. He was effectively forced to resign, taking 'the "can back" for others' (according to former BR Operations Manager Peter Rayner).[89]

No one forgot.

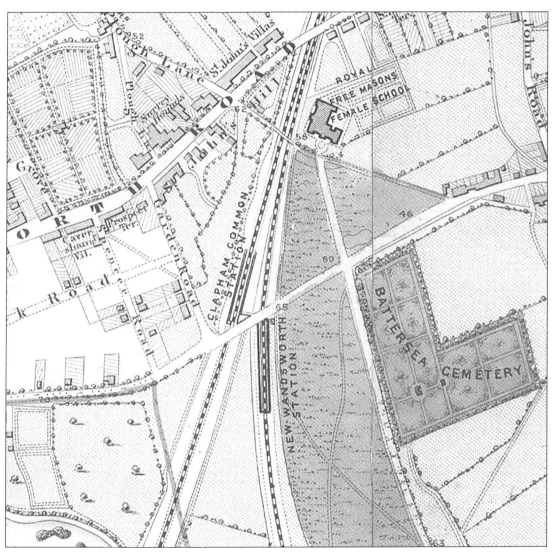

This map, by Edward Stanford, shows the Clapham area in 1862. Clapham Common station had been opened by the London & South Western Railway as 'Wandsworth' in 1838. Renamed in 1846, it closed in 1863 when Clapham Junction station opened in its place.

Passenger traction on the Southern in 1936. Here, N15 No.754 *The Green Knight* is seen at Waterloo. These impressive 4-6-0s were designed by Robert W. Urie and built between 1918 and 1927. *(Rail Photoprints Collection)*

Sir Herbert Walker strove to electrify as much of the Southern Railway as possible. But it wasn't all about main line expresses; 2-NOL electric multiple units like this one were built between 1934 and 1936 for stopping services on the South Coast and in South London. They utilised former LSWR bodies, which were lengthened and placed on new underframes. *(Colour-Rail)*

The face of Bournemouth line services in 1938, as 'Schools' class No.925 *Cheltenham* is seen at Clapham Junction with a service from the resort to Waterloo. *(Rail Photoprints – Dave Cobbe Collection (C. R. L. Coles))*

Steam locomotive development on the Southern arguably reached its height with Bulleid's 'Merchant Navy' class of Pacifics. Here 21C12 (later No.35012) *United States Line* heads west through Vauxhall with a Down express c.1948. *(Rail Photoprints)*

LONDON-
SOUTHAMPTON
& BOURNEMOUTH

ELECTRIFIED - JULY 10

MORE SPEED, MORE COMFORT, MORE TRAINS

The sane way to travel

British Rail Inter-City

BR poster heralding the coming of electric services between Waterloo and Bournemouth from 10 July 1967. This image was taken by the author at Corfe Castle on the Swanage Railway, where the poster has been preserved.

After the withdrawal of steam, Waterloo–Bournemouth services were taken over by electric multiple units like this one, seen at the Dorset resort in 1967. *(Colour-Rail (G. Pratt))*

The operational benefits of using locomotives at both ends of a train were demonstrated on the Scottish Region, which introduced accelerated services between Edinburgh and Glasgow using (mainly) pairs of Class 27 diesel-electrics in May 1971. Here, 5394 is seen at Waverley in July 1972. *(Rail Photoprints (Andrew Beavis))*

The Class 47/7s featured technology that allowed them to be driven from their own cabs or from a driving trailer at the opposite end of the train. As discussed in Chapter 3, they began to take over from the 'top-and-tail' Class 27 formations on Glasgow–Edinburgh services in October 1979. Here, 47701 *Saint Andrew* waits at Haymarket depot in the February of that year. *(Rail Photoprints (John Chalcraft))*

The collision at Polmont on 31 July 1984 led to the deaths of 13 people. The accident and its causes are described in Chapter 4. Note that the leading DBSO turned end-for-end as a result of the collision (as evidenced by the double arrow logo on the cab side door). *(Reach Publishing Services Ltd.)*

A picture of the Southern Region in the mid-1980s, exemplified by 33027 *Earl Mountbatten of Burma*, which is seen at Waterloo with the 09:10 for Exeter on 27 February 1986. *(Rail Photoprints (John A.M. Vaughan))*

The Weymouth of the pre-electrification era, complete with SR upper quadrant signal. In this view, 47536 is waiting to return to Bromsgrove with a special excursion. *(Colour-Rail (R. Siviter))*

The Weymouth of the coming electrification era, the third rail now in evidence, along with the classic Network SouthEast red lamp posts, as 33117 arrives on 25 July 1987. *(Colour-Rail (G. Goodall))*

The vibrant colours of Network SouthEast, as sported by 50023 *Howe* and a rake of Mark II carriages at Clapham on 10 June 1986. This was the day of the NSE launch, and loco and carriages will soon take their place at Waterloo for the opening ceremony. *(Colour-Rail)*

The new face of Waterloo–Weymouth services, in the form of a Class 442 'Wessex' unit. Capable of 100 mph, these were based on the Mark III carriage – a first for the Southern Region, which had favoured Mark I designs for many years (although the '442s' did reuse the traction motors of their Mark I predecessors).

A special leaflet produced by Network SouthEast to mark the start of the new electric services on the Waterloo–Weymouth route.

The light before the darkness. A leaflet produced by Network SouthEast to encourage leisure travel by rail. Summer 1988.

The level crossing collision at Lockington on 26 July 1986 led to the deaths of eight rail passengers and an 11-year-old boy travelling in a van struck by the train. *(Reach Publishing Services Ltd.)*

On 19 September 1986, two trains collided at Colwich Junction in Staffordshire. One train driver was killed. The accident highlighted the need to communicate rule changes clearly but also brought praise for the strength of the Mark III carriages involved. *(Reach Publishing Services Ltd.)*

The sad remains of the King's Cross fire of 18 November 1987, an accident that claimed 31 lives. *(London Fire Brigade / Mary Evans Picture Library)*

An Up 'Gatwick Express' service – now running under the InterCity banner – is propelled towards Clapham Junction by 73212 *Airtour Suisse*. It is November 1988. Within a month, photographers will be in the area for a much darker reason. *(Rail Photoprints (John Chalcraft))*

Under a rainy sky, NSE-liveried 47710 takes empty stock from Waterloo under the signal box at Clapham. The relay room is the flat-roofed building on the right of the gantry. *(Rail Photoprints)*

Firemen and British Rail staff cut through the wreckage of the Clapham accident in the search for survivors. *(Reach Publishing Services Ltd.)*

Heavy lifting gear was brought in to aid the clearance of the Clapham site. *(Reach Publishing Services Ltd.)*

A grimmer purpose for a Class 73 as 73129 aids the clear-up operation at Clapham. *(Colour-Rail)*

Relays in Clapham Junction 'A' Relay Room, showing track circuit relay 'DN' next to track repeater relay 'DM'. *(British Transport Police)*

Relay 'TRR DM', taken on 12 December 1988 at around 14:00. *(British Transport Police)*

Taken from an official BR booklet, the upper image shows a twin AWS magnet in the track and the receiver attached to a locomotive. The lower image shows the AWS bell and horn, as fitted inside a locomotive cab.

The Purley accident of 4 March 1989 resulted from a train passing a signal at danger. Five people were killed and six carriages left the rails before careering down an embankment in a residential area. *(Reach Publishing Services Ltd.)*

Two days after Purley, on 6 March 1989, a train passed a signal at danger at Bellgrove, in Glasgow. Two people were killed. *(Reach Publishing Services Ltd.)*

DEPARTMENT OF TRANSPORT

Investigation into the Clapham Junction Railway Accident

Anthony Hidden QC

The 'Hidden report' into the Clapham accident would also consider the causes of the Purley and Bellgrove accidents.

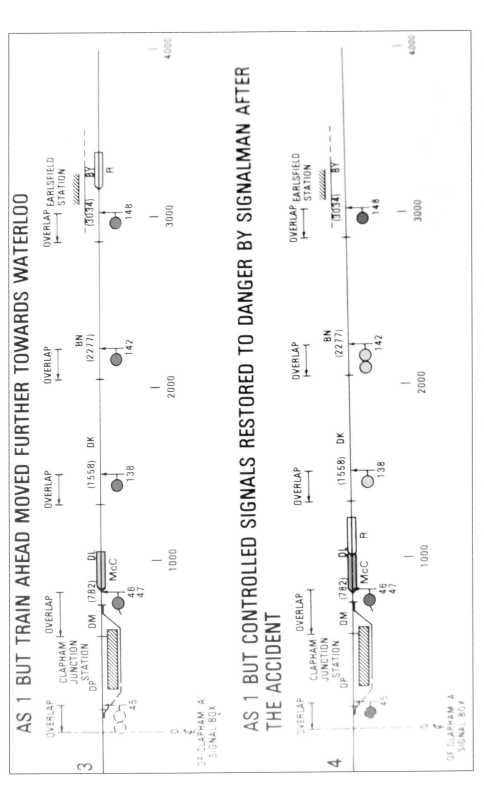

Detail from Appendix K13 of the Hidden report, showing the state of the signals just before the collision and at the point of it. See Chapter 8.

In the top diagram, all signals from 148 to 46/47 are green, showing that Driver Rolls (whose train is denoted 'R') would have thought he had a clear run, when clearly he did not. In the bottom diagram, 138 signal (the one immediately protecting the collision site) is 'single yellow'; 142 signal is on 'double yellow' and 148 signal is green. This is *after* Cotter had replaced all signals to danger.

SAFETY PLAN

1991

British Rail's first Safety Plan, published in February 1991 after consultation with Du Pont Safety Management Systems. See Chapter 20.

Above: Scene of devastation at Southall on 19 September 1997. *(Reach Publishing Services Ltd.)*

Right: The rescue operation continues in the wake of the Ladbroke Grove accident of 5 October 1999. *(London Fire Brigade / Mary Evans Picture Library)*

The Hatfield accident of 17 October 2000 killed four people and led to a series of crippling speed restrictions across the network while the integrity of the track was checked. (*Reach Publishing Services Ltd.*)

The collision at Waterloo on 15 August 2017 demonstrated the need to remember the learning from Clapham, as Simon French – then Chief Inspector of the Branch – made clear in the report. (*Rail Accident Investigation Branch*)

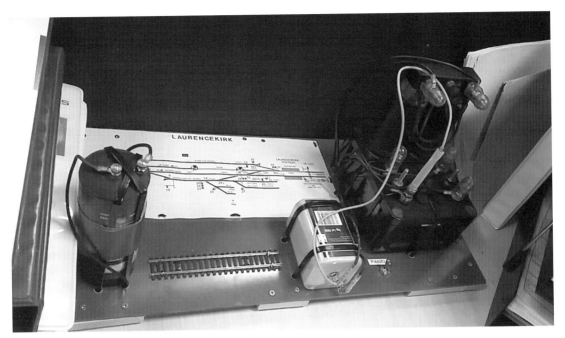

With many new, young testers entering the fold, and mindful of the generation that has passed since Clapham, Neil Massey, VolkerRail's Senior Test Engineer, produced this working simulation of the 'Clapham wiring' to demonstrate what happened to it on that fateful day in 1988. *(Neil Massey)*

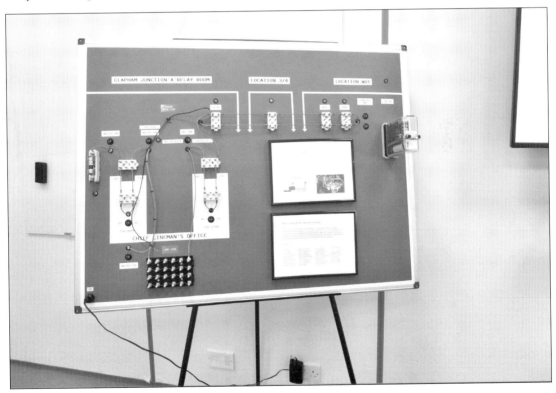

The Clapham wiring model made by Siemens Chief Engineer Andy Stringer, which the author has operated. A sobering experience.

The memorial to those involved in the Clapham accident. *(Wiki Commons / Edgepedia)*

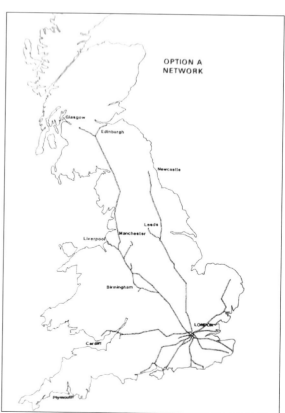

OPTION A
NETWORK

Serpell's "Option A".

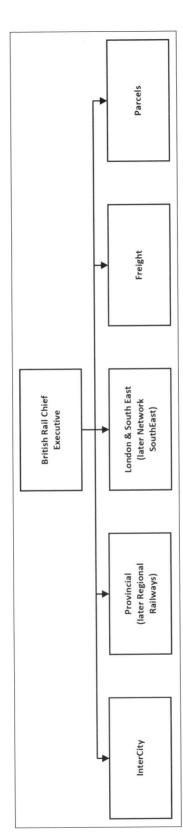

BR's original British Rail business sector structure.

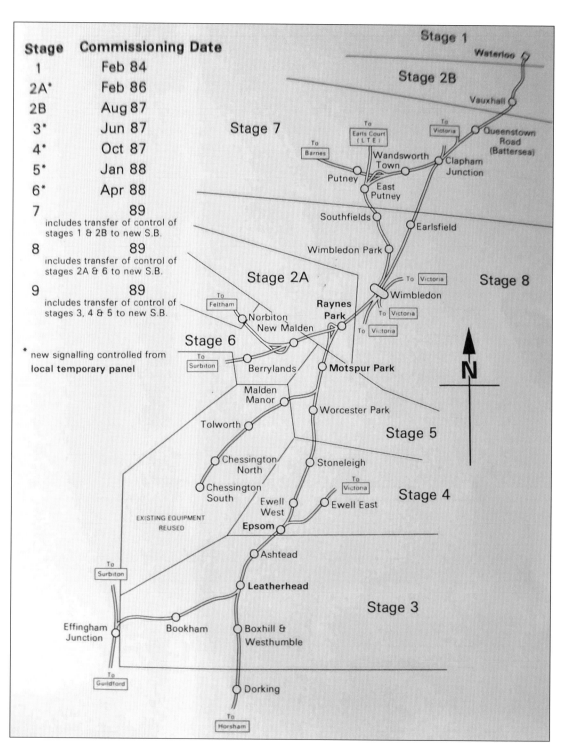

Stage	Commissioning Date
1	Feb 84
2A*	Feb 86
2B	Aug 87
3*	Jun 87
4*	Oct 87
5*	Jan 88
6*	Apr 88
7	89

includes transfer of control of
stages 1 & 2B to new S.B.

8   89
includes transfer of control of
stages 2A & 6 to new S.B.

9   89
includes transfer of control of
stages 3, 4 & 5 to new S.B.

* new signalling controlled from
local temporary panel

The planned stages of the WARS project (from the Hidden Report, Appendix K5).

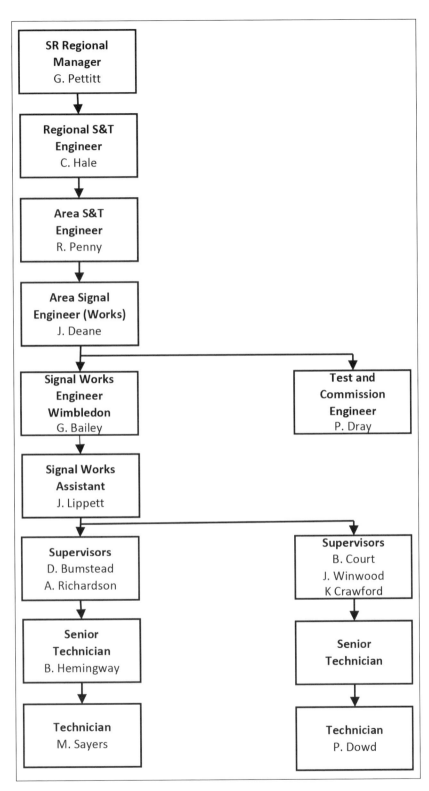

BR's organisational structure after the May 1988 reorganisation and as at 12 December 1988.

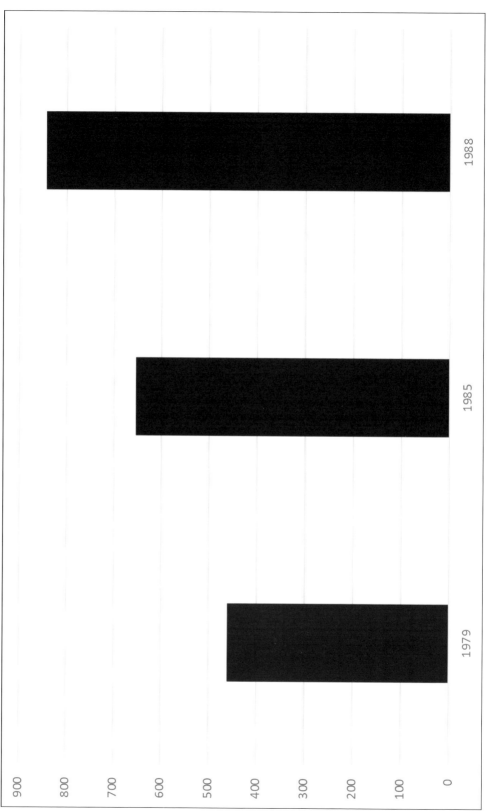

Signals passed at danger: 1979-1988 - cited in Gourvish 2, p.356.

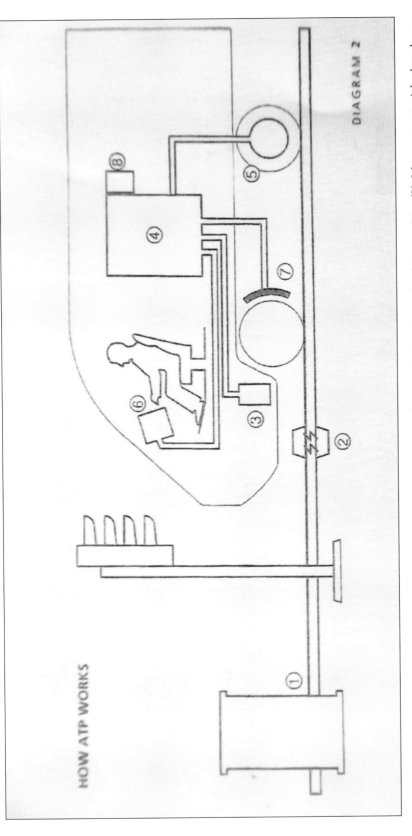

HOW ATP WORKS

DIAGRAM 2

With ATP, lineside equipment (1) supplies information on speed limits, gradients and signals to a track transmitter (2). Messages are picked up by an antenna (3) on the train and passed to an on-board computer (4). This computer already has details of the length, weight and braking characteristics of the train and is fed from the tachometer (5) with information on the train's speed and position. The computer calculates the safe speed for the train and monitors the driver's handling of the train throughout the journey. If the driver fails to respond correctly to the information displayed in the cab (6), the computer activates the brakes (7). The 'black-box' data recorder (8) on the train records all the relevant information.

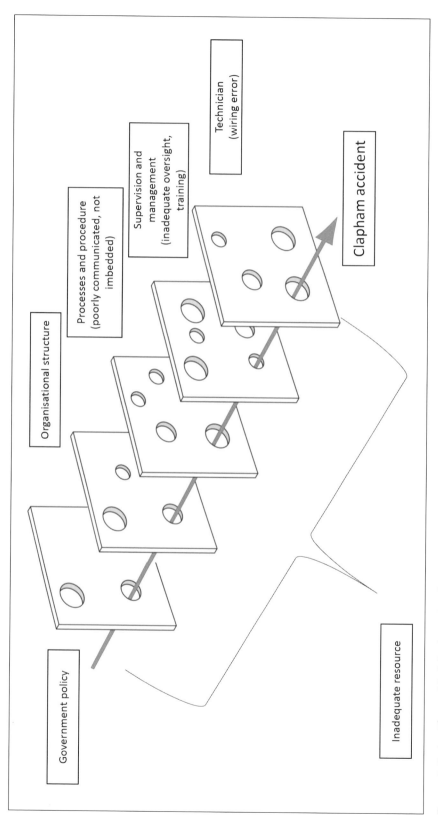

Organisational structure

Processes and procedure
(poorly communicated, not
imbedded)

Supervision and
management
(inadequate oversight,
training)

Technician
(wiring error)

Government policy

Inadequate resource

Clapham accident

Reason's Swiss Cheese Model adapted to the Clapham accident.

PART 3:

THE ELEMENTS DEFEATED

Chapter 20

What Was Done?

If it were done, when 'tis done, then 'twere well it were done quickly.
Shakespeare, *Macbeth*

Eleven days and eight minutes. Eight minutes from Waterloo to Clapham. Eleven days in the job. In November 1988, Maurice Holmes, an experienced railwayman, experienced railway *director* indeed, was appointed British Rail's first Director of Safety. He had been in post just eleven days when Clapham occurred. As we saw in Chapter 16, back in January – when still Director of Operations – he had written to the Joint Managing Director (Railways) to voice his concerns that 'past high safety standards [were] starting to be eroded by a change in the railway culture'. His own appointment was part of the solution, but in the same month he wrote his letter, BR also adopted a new Total Quality Management (TQM) initiative. Seen by some as a reaction to the November 1987 King's Cross Underground fire, its development pre-dated that tragedy, followed on from sectorisation, and was intended (as Hidden would paraphrase) to 'balance the humanitarian and the commercial approach to the concept of safety' by improving the calibre of work done, improving communications between management and staff, tightening the procedures used and the working practices involved, and by focusing on company-wide training in 'quality awareness'. One might add that it was also about shoring up the crumbling edge of which Parker had warned back in the 1970s.

Quality Management

Hidden may have recommended that BR 'continue to press ahead' with TQM, but by July 1988, some five months before the accident, policy documents had already been produced on the provision of signalling, the problem of signalling maintenance and the implementation of TQM throughout the whole S&T section. It had long been decided to appoint Clifford Hale to the post of Quality Manager, but it is bitterly ironic that he took up his new duties on the day Clapham occurred.[90] 'Had the quality initiative been in place and work within the S&T Department been certified as meeting British Standard BS5750,' wrote Hidden, 'the major weaknesses which allowed circumstances to combine in such a way as to cause the … accident might well have been eradicated'. Indeed, instructions would arguably have been more clearly drafted, staff working to laid-down standards would have been more aware of their own responsibilities (and those of others), and the quality of the installation work and the testing process would have been regularly reviewed.

BR's aim had been to introduce TQM at all levels within five years. Hidden noted that the task would need 'a major commitment by senior management'. To be fair, BR already knew that, and by the end of 1989 a major programme across all sectors, regions and functions had seen 600 managers trained, with many more to come.[91] Yet TQM itself was soon to change. In September 1988, the Board had debated future organisational development and opted to enhance sector control further. As Reid would tell both Channon and Parkinson, sectorisation *per se* had 'run its course', a study by consultants Coopers & Lybrand recommending that BR simplify and decentralise on market-based business lines. The result was the Organising for Quality initiative, which was known colloquially as 'OforQ' (what else?), and which led to a greater focus on business-led 'profit centres' within the sectors. In time, it would also (to quote Gourvish) involve 'the identification of very clear lines of responsibility for safety … validated by [a] Safety & Standards Directorate'.

That, of course, was some way off, and while all the necessary meetings were being held and all the necessary arrangements were being made, many other streams of work were flowing. Most involved the main focus of Hidden's recommendations: the S&T department. In April 1989, its newly appointed director, Ken Burrage, recognised the need to restore 'steadiness and self-confidence' to his management team. And that team had much to do. The fatigue question raised by Hemingway's near thirteen-week stint, for example, which was alarming enough for Hidden to recommend that BR monitor its work patterns, led first to the immediate reduction of overtime being worked by key S&T staff. Commissioning times were also rescheduled, while 'interim monitoring arrangements' were quickly established, along with a working party to develop criteria for what were considered acceptable levels of working time.[92] Soon, BR would be focussing on how 'progressively [to] reduce the amount of excessive overtime worked by front line staff with safety responsibilities'.[93] Soon it would be focussing on the bedrock of safety – training.

BR's own inquiry had already recognised the need to 'ensure that allocated S&T staff [were] capable of undertaking the tasks allocated to them'.[94] Training in S&T was a bit of a rolling requirement. An agreement with the National Union of Railwaymen (NUR) meant that Assistant Technicians, Technicians, Leading Technicians, Senior

Technicians and Technician Officers were not recruited from outside the railway, but relied on an internal promotion system. The trouble was, BR's competitors for this kind of expertise *did* recruit externally – *largely from BR*. This created a 'continual demand for training of those who fill the gap created by such recruitment either by joining BR or rising within its ranks to a higher grade'. BR reported that it was 'monitoring and forecasting' the wastage and recruitment of skilled S&T staff.[95] It also set about merging the wage and salaried staff grades and increased the basic pay rates by 25 per cent.

Hidden clarified the need to give technical training to technical staff, refresher courses to installers at intervals of not more than five years, training certification to testers and regular reviews to make sure courses retained their relevance (Recommendations 14-17). BR reviewed its technical training courses and established 'systems for ensuring and maintaining [the] competency of [its] testers within the S&T Department' soon after the accident. It also introduced simulators and interactive videos to take the courses away from the desk and classroom to something closer to the railway itself.[96] In addition, a new training organisation was established for S&T, while the recommended 'refreshers' drew upon a suite of new handbooks.[97] Later still, and mindful of the fact that BR's own measures were not necessarily 'sufficient to restore the credibility of S&T', the Institution of Railway Signal Engineers (IRSE) produced its own licensing scheme. Launched in January 1994 by none other than Hidden himself, it covered (*inter alia*) installation, maintenance, testing, design, project engineering and engineering management. By September 2013, some 12,000 licences would be issued.[98]

The need to cut back and insulate redundant wiring was – like many points raised by Hidden in this area – re-asserted as soon as BR's own investigators had revealed it to be required.[99] However, to make sure that testing would spot its absence in the future, the company also introduced a national Signalling Works Testing Handbook to clarify 'those tests which must be done prior to commissioning', and whose instructions were thenceforth subject to 'regular review and revision when necessary'.[100] Similarly, a Signalling Design Handbook tightened up Design Office procedures for producing, issuing and amending documents to ensure that all working drawings were both complete and accurate. The Design Office Handbook would also be enhanced by implementing BS5750 standards in the signalling design offices at Croydon and Glasgow (Recommendation 3).

Training and Technology

All these handbooks, all these procedures, policies, edicts and instructions would only be any good, of course, if those who needed to get them, got them, read them and understood them. As we saw in Chapter 10, instructions SL-53 (*Testing of New and Altered Signalling*) and SI-16 (*Termination of Signalling Cables and Wires*) fell some way short of this need, so Hidden recommended that BR devise effective distribution systems, which would make sure all who received such instructions – including anyone who moved to a new position – were appraised on their knowledge of them every two years. This related to Recommendations 12 and 13. In response to Recommendation 13 specifically, BR wrote that steps had been 'immediately taken' in S&T to make sure key instructions were being understood. In Mechanical Engineering, all supervisors and managers were having to sign a declaration that relevant instructions had been read and understood. A similar edict had been issued by Civil Engineering, while Operations had developed 'a positive system for individuals to be recertificated' following the completion of biennial examinations.[101]

Communication was clearly vital, but though BR made these moves, and though it engaged none other than James Reason to look into 'the large part human error plays in incidents and accidents of all types', it knew the real answer lay in technology.[102] As well as reviewing its manual circulation procedures, it therefore opted to develop a computerised database for maintaining records of both document distribution and document receipt. By February 1991, work was 'well advanced', with two pilot schemes due for introduction that April prior to 'progressive implementation throughout the industry'.[103]

Not that this was the sort of technology Holmes had been thinking of when he had written that he 'would not like a major disaster with loss of life to be the reason that forced British Rail to invest in modern safety aids'. Modern safety aids at that time included cab-to-shore radios, transmitted via the National Radio Network (NRN), which had come to Euston in 1977, but which had developed more speedily after Polmont. In *that* case, it would have allowed the presence of the cow that was struck with such fatal consequence to have been reported immediately and not at the next station. In the specific case of Clapham, Holmes's successor as Director of Operations, Ivor Warburton, pointed out that 'if the driver of an earlier train had reported an irregularity, the danger was unlikely to be realised immediately because the correct track circuit indications continued to be given in the signal box'. So, if McClymont had reported the irregularity he did indeed see at WF138 signal on the morning of the accident via cab radio and not a signal post telephone, the signaller, Cotter, would probably still have told him the indication on his panel suggested all to be well.

There were other issues to consider too, including the fact that NRN, while cost-effective and wide-ranging, was unsecure, heavily dependent on BR's telephone network, and could not be linked to signalling areas. This made it unsuitable for intensive use on busy suburban lines like those out of Waterloo. The alternative, known as Cab Secure Radio (CSR), was trialled on the suburban lines out of King's Cross and the Bedford to St Pancras route in the late 1970s, becoming mandatory on services worked by the driver alone – indeed it was one of the safety requirements agreed between BR and the Railway Inspectorate for this kind of operation. CSR was direct, more reliable, and interlocked with the equipment in the signal box. It was also incompatible with NRN.

At the time, there were 'difficulties, first with the Home Office and subsequently with the Department of Trade & Industry in securing a sufficient allocation of frequency channels'. As an interim measure, it was decided to adapt NRN for drivers, a move that led to the Overlay Radio Network (ORN), which featured an emergency button that could be used to contact the Regional Control Room, from where calls could be made to the relevant signal box. According to Clive Kessell, then BR's Assistant Director (Telecommunications), it was 'not perfect, although it did 'prevent a number of accidents […] from happening'.

The other side of the equation was of course cost, exactly as it had been for WARS. Hidden was concerned that cab radios might have had to '[take] their place in a list of other safety enhancing projects, competing with them for funds'. He said that, fortunately, this was 'not borne out … by the rest of the evidence'. It is hard not to see naivety in this comment, but in the event (and before Hidden had published) BR committed itself 'to extend its plan for the introduction of cab radios and to quicken the timescale to ensure that all units [were] fitted by 1992'. By February 1990, it was reporting – in response to Recommendation 43 – that the programme of fitting radios to its main line locomotive fleet was 'virtually complete', that 'urgent consideration' was being given to using 'Cellnet telephones as an interim system of driver-to-shore communication', and that a trial for the latter was being planned on the London–Tilbury–Southend line.[104]

In addition, Hidden reiterated ASLEF's recommendation that 'all radio communication … be recorded both to ensure that the system is not abused and to provide an accurate record of communication in case of any incident'. This idea fed into BR's pre-existing policy to introduce on-train data recorders, or tachographs, to all new stock, and retrofit them progressively to all existing stock expected to have a long life. Data recorders could not of course prevent accidents, but the information collected – train speed, signal aspect and so on – would offer significant benefits to accident investigation. Hidden wanted the equipment afforded 'a higher priority' than BR had proposed hitherto, and while accepting the recommendation, the company did point out that the equipment specification had first to be prepared.

By February 1990, BR was 'committed to the principle of data recorders and [was] assessing the fastest means of introducing an on-train data recorder to all traction'.[105] By February 1991, they were starting to be received, being destined for the new Class 319 and 321 electric multiple units.[106] They were also destined for the record-breaking Class 442s. The latter were indeed 'a significant advance in passenger comfort and in journey times', but they were not without problems. As the Department of Transport reported, 'the power doors, of a design new to British Railways, proved unreliable in service and several incidents were reported where trains were able to travel at speed with some of the doors open'.[107] Thankfully no one fell from them. Subsequently, the door controls were modified to reduce the risk.

Structural Integrity

Unfortunately, there were not 442s enough to provide a full service, meaning many expresses on the Waterloo–Weymouth route remained in the hands of older Mark I stock. All the 32 carriages involved in the Clapham accident had been of that type and no-one who had been travelling in the first third of the Poole train's leading vehicle had survived, 'compression of the passenger space [being] the cause of most of the fatal injuries'. Hidden added that the units involved at Purley and Bellgrove were from the same family, those at Purley dating from 1967 and 1970 (Classes 423 and 421/2 respectively), those at Bellgrove dating from 1960 (Class 303).[108] There was, said Hidden, 'a clear need to minimise the risk of deaths and injuries in railway accidents by the improvement of collision resistance in rolling stock and more particularly in passenger stock on intensely worked routes'.

Of course, rolling stock, and rolling stock strength, had improved over time, and while the Mark Is might have been seen as deficient by 1989, when new they were considered a great advance on the types that preceded them. Indeed, Lieutenant-Colonel Wilson, who investigated the Harrow & Wealdstone accident, noted that while the fatality count had been high, the collision demonstrated the Mark I's superior strength, specifically their all-steel welded bodies, which were mounted on 200-ton end-load resistant underframes.[109] Two were in one of the trains involved; both 'kept their form as integral structures without very severe disturbance of the internal partitions and fittings'; both were 'nearly twice as strong as any of the [pre-nationalisation] designs'.[110] By contrast, many of those older designs had wooden bodies, which, while not reduced to 'matchwood' (as Rolt might have described it), certainly fared less well, two of them being 'shattered as they were telescoped together'.

The Mark II design improved on the Mark Is, having a rigid body and no separate underframe, while the Mark IIIs – with their aircraft-like, all-steel 'monocoque' construction – were an improvement again. The Southern Region, however, had persisted with Mark Is, the last of which appeared in 1974 to meet a significant timetable enhancement that saw hourly fast and semi-fast trains added to its service. Existing three-coach trailer sets were strengthened to four, and eight more REP tractor units were built. The former were rebuilds of earlier Mark I stock, but the REPs were constructed new, and were the final Mark I bodies built for BR. Later commentators felt that, in eschewing the Mark II design for so long, the Southern had been 'constrained by earlier principles'. The truth would have been more closely aligned to economy, just as the Bournemouth electrification scheme had been in the 1960s.

By the late 1980s, the situation had changed, the 442s having been constructed to the stronger Mark III standards (despite utilising the traction motors and electrical control gear from the earlier REPs). Only four had been available for the start of the new timetable on 16 May 1988. How might the death count at Clapham have been lessened had they been rostered for the 06:14 from Poole – a 'Class 1' express? BR's publicity material for the 442s had promised 'an hourly service to London starting at Poole', after all, so it is possible that one could have been involved in the accident had delivery and availability allowed. BR's inquiry, though, while recognising that the Mark Is had not been 'designed to modern agreed international requirements', felt it was 'for question' whether Mark III-type bodies 'would have behaved much differently in the case of this particular collision'.[111] It probably *was* 'for question', but the superior performance of the Mark IIIs involved in the Colwich accident – specifically the fact that no passenger was killed – made it a question worth asking.[112]

But of course it wasn't just the Southern; across the network, BR had a huge number of Mark I vehicles, which had around a decade of useful economic life left to go. Hidden welcomed BR's forthcoming million-pound research programme aimed at testing and improving the design. The work would consider coupler strength, override protection and 'enhanced passenger safety'. It was to be completed by April 1991 (and would eventually lead to the passing of the Railways and Other Transport Systems Approval of Works, Plant and Equipment Regulations 1994, commonly known as ROTS).

Train Protection

Regardless of how strong your trains are, it is arguably better if they can be prevented from colliding in the first place. Though not a feature of Clapham, as we have seen, trains passing signals at danger were causal to the Purley, Bellgrove and Colwich accidents. It was a trend that had been rising, the numbers of SPADs having jumped from 460 in 1979 to 653 in 1985 and 843 in 1988.[113] In 1986, BR had asked the Royal Holloway College to assist its Research Division to conduct an investigation into causation. The Chief Inspecting Officer of Railways had – in his annual reports for 1985, 1986 and 1988 – been pushing for the adoption of something better, something more proactive than AWS, which was essentially an *advisory* technology, whose efficacy was being challenged by the use of increasingly modern trains on an increasingly higher-speed network. And by this time, something better *was* available, something that was capable of automatically restricting the speed of a train on the approach to a signal at danger.

A number of these Automatic Train Protection (ATP) systems were in use across Europe and in Japan, but none was considered suitable for buying straight off the shelf. Instead, BR needed a modified system that was 'capable of operating with total integrity in BR's intensive traffic conditions including a mix of fast and stopping passenger services and freight trains using the same track and signalling'. As 'BR also had less space on its trains to fit the ATP equipment without major alterations', it had to be suitable in this sense too.

Earlier in 1988, Holmes had been part of a delegation that saw ATP in action during a visit to Sweden. That October, he and Ken Hodgson (as Director of S&T Engineering) submitted a proposal to the Board that £140 million be spent over ten years on a bespoke system that would cover about 80 per cent of passenger miles run. Signed off the following month, Chris Green was asked to take the plan forward. Until this point, it had been thought that the safety advantages of ATP were not sufficient to justify the investment, as the project would not meet the 7 per cent rate of return required by the Department of Transport. BR therefore tried to calculate the savings in accident costs that ATP might have made had it existed between 1970 and 1986. Using the £500,000 figure the Department applied when assessing the cost to society of a road death gave a saving of between £6 and £10 million a year. These were rough figures, which – it had been felt – were not worth pursuing further.

Nevertheless, Holmes and Hodgson concluded that, if given high enough priority, the ATP project could be completed in five years. Although BR had since adopted a policy of implementation over a *ten*-year period, Hidden pushed for full implementation within the shorter timeframe (Recommendation 46). Green's outline appraisal of February 1989 suggested the capital cost of the scheme to be some £250 million, although head of InterCity Dr John Prideaux felt £400 million to be more realistic. With a similar irony to that which surrounded the introduction of AWS, two days after Purley, and on the same day as Bellgrove, BR's Investment Committee authorised £1 million to be spent on developing ATP and a provision of £17.4 million to be made for it in BR's five-year investment plan. Both accidents would have been prevented by the new equipment. By February 1990, though, BR was able to report that two contractors were to be appointed for two pilot schemes. Test commissioning for the first of these was scheduled to start in May 1991.[114]

BR might not have been in a position to relax, as its latest advertisements were exhorting its passengers to do, but it was perhaps getting there. The going, of course, was not going to be easy, and there was one man destined not to see the manifold outcomes of all this effort. For him, it was time to go.

Chapter 21

Endgame

'Change' is scientific, 'progress' is ethical; change is indubitable, whereas progress is a matter of controversy.

Bertrand Russell,
Unpopular Essays, 1950

1 April 1990. Sir Robert Reid had been on the railway for 43 years, and now it was about to end. When electrification came to the Bournemouth line, he'd been working for the Scottish Region in Glasgow; when the 47/7s came to Edinburgh, he was on the Board as its main marketing man; by the time Polmont occurred, he'd taken over from Parker as chairman.

Seen by some to have presided over a 'golden age', there was no denying that the last fifteen months had cast a pall. That short period had not only seen three major accidents, but also an acrimonious dispute with the unions over pay that had brought 'chaos and complete closure to the network', and a fraud inquiry, which had led to the resignations of several senior managers, after their improper acceptance of 'inducements' from Plasser, the track machine manufacturer.[115]

Reid was under no illusion, of course, and had expressed his views in no uncertain terms in a speech to the Chartered Institute of Transport on 8 January. He began by presenting the positive aspects of the last full financial year of his term of office, 1988/89, and comparing it with his first year of 1983. Thus, the 10 per cent rise in passenger numbers was vaunted, InterCity's £57 million profit (from a £200 million loss in 1983) was heralded and Railfreight's operating surplus of £69.4 million was described as 'the best result for a decade'. Furthermore, the Public Service Obligation had been cut 'by over 50 per cent in real terms', while 'the annual level of investment [had] doubled'. There were also 72 more stations, 2,000 new carriages and 110 new locomotives.

After expanding on his own career, describing Beeching, Serpell and the inception, need for and role of sectorisation, he outlined the lessons he and BR had learned. Among them was the point that, while change may be continuous, a large organisation 'can only absorb large leaps infrequently'. Fiennes, who had died in 1985, would have been delighted.

Reid also recognised the importance of communication, 'listening and telling', the need to track developments through analysis, and of course the need to keep safety at the 'top of the railway agenda'. 'There must be no repeat of the Clapham disaster,' he said, but the 'only answer' was 'high standards, efficient systems and constant vigilance'. With this in mind 'Safety Audit' had become a Board-level function and training had received the level of recognition it required.[116]

The speech finished with Reid outlining what he saw as BR's priorities for the coming decade. He looked forward to the coming of the Channel Tunnel, to gaining Parliamentary approval for the proposed Paddington–Heathrow Airport services and the CrossRail link between the former (and future) Great Western terminus and Liverpool Street. He did see that his successor '[might] not be quite so fortunate managing an industry so dependent on the British economy as [he had] been'. The downturn in the early 1980s, and the miners' strike of 1984/5, had 'knocked [BR] badly'; it recovered 'because the economy did'. But would BR's reorganisation 'enable [BR] to do just as well in a period of much slower economic growth'? Reid thought it would, but there can be no denying that he left BR battered and bruised (though perhaps not as bruised as Parker).

Meet the New Boss …

Reid's replacement was the former Chairman and Chief Executive of Shell UK … Bob Reid. Parkinson had wanted an industrialist, but this second Reid did not come cheap, drawing a starting salary almost double that of his predecessor.[117] He took over the helm fully and formally in October 1990. He said he was personally committed to change, although – culturally – this was already on the way. In 1989 – during the preparations of the evidence for Hidden – the Board had appointed consultants Arthur D. Little, Bridget Hutter of Wolfson College, Oxford, and American firm Du Pont to look at safety management on the West Coast Main Line, an approach endorsed by Hidden's Recommendation 38.[118]

James Catmur, now a director at JC and Associates, but then with Arthur D. Little, was 'petrified' as he observed an S&T team working without following the Rule Book. 'As I recall,' he says, 'I think they did comply with one rule. I still wonder if that was normal practice or them trying to scare me (they succeeded)'. As Catmur confirms, the Arthur D. Little report 'was instrumental in the move to formal safety management systems and risk assessment'. Du Pont also highlighted how safety at BR was 'compartmentalised', safety of the system being separate from safety of the staff. Management too were often more reactive than proactive, although the Safety Directorate established by Maurice Holmes in 1988 wasn't really resourced enough to be anything else. Du Pont made a number of recommendations, including the need for a written safety policy, effective monitoring and training, and an audit programme. This, BR's first *Safety Plan*, was published in February 1991. Issued to every member of staff, from shunter to driver, signalling technician, buffet car attendant, manager, supervisor and director, it paid particular attention to organisational issues, investment and working methods. 'At the concluding stages of the [Clapham] inquiry,' wrote Reid II, 'my predecessor said … "absolute safety is our aim" … I wish to repeat my personal commitment to that objective'.[119] He recognised that the changes required to achieve this would 'touch every one of our staff, as well as many members of the wider community in which we operate'.

The flavour of the early safety courses given on the East Coast Main Line around this time has been described by former signaller (and later trainer) Richard Clarke, who admitted that the going was not always easy. On the one hand, as he says, the programme 'was a huge success as many employees were unaware of the potential dangers they were exposed to in their workplace', but on the other 'it was hard to deliver the section on "reporting of near misses" with conviction. After all, railwaymen had spent most of their working life covering up for near misses! This new approach was perceived as "snitching" and many of those attending would never report a near miss if one of their colleagues would be dropped in it!' It took 'some convincing on the part of the trainer that we were now a "no blame" culture'.[120]

It was an important point to make, as it was part of the ongoing drive for quality. One key delivery mechanism here, with links to business management and the quality initiative, was the Safety Panel – an investment committee chaired by Board member David Rayner. It had a wide-ranging remit (and a considerable budget) to identify and prioritise schemes which needed a push and/or an injection of funds and was backed by the new sectors (Richard George represented Intercity, Chris Tibbitts represented Network SouthEast, Martin Shrubsole acted for Provincial, Aidan Nelson for Freight, Charles Belcher for Parcels and Michael Woods for European Passenger Services). A trail-blazing feature was the development of the first serious attempt to provide a financial benefit for planned safety investments, developed by David Maidment, later the founder of the Railway Children charity. This allowed schemes like ATP, data recorders, radio communications, and crashworthiness improvements to be appraised on a common numerical basis. The process would eventually lead to the creation of the Safety Risk Model, under Railway Safety (see page 172). At the same time, those working on big investment projects, like the Eurostar stations and links to the Channel Tunnel, noticed a major change to the way they had to work, every new scheme or significant change having to include both a business case and a safety impact analysis.

The trade press soon picked up on the concept of 'quality'. *Rail* had said it was an 'in-word' that was 'elusive', but should not be 'so perfect that it cannot be mass produced'. *Modern Railways* said (a bit later) that 'the totem of Quality is frequently worshipped, but less commonly understood', while Roger Ford kicked off his customary analysis by likening the Big New Thing to 'bull', such was the level of 'pious generalisation, larded with buzz words and acronyms' that seemed to surround it.[121] For Ford though, at least Brian Burdsall, BR's first appointed Director, Quality 'displayed a heartening relationship with the real world'. But then, BR had entered this arena because of a very 'real world' problem …

OfQ, of course, was a wide-reaching initiative intended to cover everything, but if you're going to cover everything you need information, you need data. The data collected on wrong-side failures had been found to be deficient, but while BR brought in a system for monitoring, reviewing and classifying them more assiduously than before, the SPADs at Purley and Bellgrove confirmed that there was a bigger picture to try to bring into focus (Recommendation 25).[122] Before Clapham, there had been no central collation of incident-related statistics, bar those gathered by the Railway Inspectorate. BR recognised that accurate monitoring was vital in spotting trends and forming risk assessments. As a result, it launched the British Rail Incident Monitoring System (BRIMS) in 1990, which – in line with most systems of this type – did not work satisfactorily at first. The Board took steps to improve it in 1993, but realised that safety was not just about evaluating data, it was about valuing people too.

Burdsall recognised the same loyal workforce that Hidden had done, but also knew that while 'incredibly committed', they thought some of their managers were 'absolute rubbish'.[123] Hidden's report agreed that BR management was deficient, but just retraining supervisors, managers and directors was not going to be enough – morale was clearly going to be key, and not just at the front line. Some critics cited Fiennes again and felt that OfQ was dividing operations from engineering and introducing too much complexity. It would have been hard enough to get an engineer to see and understand an operator's point of view (and vice versa) as it was. Then again, it still is.

Among those who would have agreed was Peter Rayner, for whom OfQ was implemented ruthlessly and meant 'managers had no time to look after the railway'.[124] Among them too, Ken Burrage, Director of Signal & Telecommunications Engineering, who expressed his concern that the Board's OfQ working parties were pressing on, in spite of S&T's 'current operations, the investment programme and the major initiatives on quality and safety'.[125] For him, it was more important to improve his directorate's management of safety before it was handed over to any New World. Given Hidden's focus on S&T, it's easy to see why he felt like that. Others perhaps agreed, Burrage getting his way in the sense that regional S&T engineers were able to function much as they had hitherto and the Croydon HQ remained active until July 1992.

By this time, the WARS scheme had finally been completed, its new Wimbledon signalling centre having taken over the final Waterloo-Nine Elms section on 2 April 1991. By this time, too, the in-cab radio situation had moved on to the point at which all InterCity locomotives and around 60 per cent of freight locomotives had been fitted with the equipment needed to interface with the National Radio Network. A £9-million plan to supply Provincial (known as Regional Railways from 1989) had been due for completion by the end of the year.[126] In the event, the latter was afforded a low priority status and was not completed until 1994/95. Worse than this, though, was the state of the £46-million scheme to fit the Cab Secure Radio system more suited to the intensively worked suburban lines of Network SouthEast.

The plan had been to fit all NSE cabs and lines by 1996/97, but because of a recession in the early 1990s (primarily caused by high-interest rates, falling house prices and an overvalued exchange rate), the project stalled and by 1993 only 55 per cent of NSE's actual network had been enhanced.[127] Several options were considered, but the favourite involved fitting CSR to 'high-risk' routes only, leaving the outer suburban reaches with NRN. In 1994, this meant that, while most of NSE's trains had been fitted with CSR, their effectiveness was limited as there were not enough 'base stations' for the system to work across the entire NSE area. On the other hand, where the base stations were absent, there *was* NRN, but no trains equipped to use it. One of the latter areas was the Uckfield branch. BR announced its decision to fit CSR, but did it in December 1994, three days before the inquiry into a fatal collision on that line, at Cowden, had opened. Though caused by a SPAD, the resulting report noted that Cowden could have been prevented by CSR, as the signaller was aware of the situation and could have alerted the drivers of both trains, both of whom would have been able to have stopped 'about a mile and a half apart'.[128]

The Rise of ATP

Cowden – like Clapham, Purley, and Bellgrove – featured Mark I rolling stock. By the time the research on Mark Is had been prepared

scheme', and duly added a further £400 million to the limit.[136] In the event, an EFL figure of £255 million was agreed for safety in 1991/92, followed by £180 million in 1992/93. But this did not mean there was going to be enough money to make ATP widely available; in early discussions on establishing the EFL for 1993/94 and 1994/95, BR was told bluntly that the Department of Transport 'could not support the planned expenditure on [it] for those years'.

Unfortunately, Hidden had also recommended (48) the government and BR conduct 'a thorough study of investment appraisal procedures so that a financial value could be put on safety'. Thus in 1994, BR carried out a cost-benefit analysis of the whole ATP project. This showed a 'cost per equivalent fatality avoided' of £13.9 million, based on a full fitment cost, which had risen from £380 million (as quoted by Hidden) to £475 million.[137] As this was way above the level seen as justified by both the Health and Safety Executive (HSE) and the government, ATP was ruled out, leaving its two pilot schemes stranded, thereby showing the complex relationship between the public expectation of absolute safety and the Treasury requirement for value for money. The moral perhaps is "be careful what you wish for".

BR's attention had since been knocked off course by another change coming its way. In April 1992, John Major's re-elected Conservative government returned to an idea Nicholas Ridley had mooted with Thatcher in 1986, one of Major's pre-election promises having been to sell BR off – even though, to quote Gourvish, the organisation at this point 'represented the full flowering of the business-led, sector management concept ... introduced on a modest scale in 1982'. All right, overtime remained endemic, all right, it still had a lot of Mark I stock, had not introduced ATP quickly enough, or on-train (data) monitoring recorders (OTMR), CSR, or NRN. And all right, it charged its customers too much and allowed occasional idiocies like

Railfreight drivers refusing to rescue failed passenger trains as it was not their sector's business. Every BR-era rail employee the author has spoken to about this believes these problems would have been sorted out had sectorisation been given more time to bed in. Yet, even with these issues, it still offered the country a more streamlined, customer-focused, integrated organisation.

In the five years since Clapham, BR had 'achieved a considerable amount in raising awareness about safety, improving information systems and providing the organisational base for a modern health and safety policy'. And now BR, its OfQ initiative, safety organisation and new safety focus, were to be dismantled. The irony is that the changes brought in to deal with safety post-Clapham actually facilitated the organisation's own destruction, as they introduced cross-sector trading, track access charging and many other things that typify good business practice. In short, they had helped the process of restructuring and privatisation to be implemented in a fairly controlled, professional manner.

So, again, to 1 April; 1 April 1994, on which the Railways Act 1993 came into effect, allowing Railtrack, as infrastructure owner, to be severed from BR.[138] It was the culmination of a reorganisation way beyond the A&O III initiative of May 1988, which would see the creation of three rolling stock leasing companies, three technical engineering support companies, several infrastructure maintenance units, several operators and a number of track renewals units. In short, one company became over 100 separate businesses (and a fair few acronyms).

It would not be without consequence.

Chapter 22

Brave New World?

We must accept human error as inevitable, and design around that fact.

Donald Berwick,
British Medical Journal, 2001

Although a generally safe railway was handed over when Railtrack took control of the track and signalling at the start of privatisation in 1994, the Clapham accident had seen the British Railways Board fined £250,000 for failing to ensure the safety of passengers and staff.[139] The prosecution had been brought by the Railway Inspectorate, which had recently become part of the Health & Safety Executive (HSE). The involvement of the latter arguably brought more scrutiny to railway safety at a time when safety in general was being scrutinised, this being the era – to reiterate – that saw the Bradford City fire (1985), the sinking of the *Herald of Free Enterprise* at Zeebrugge (1987), the King's Cross Underground fire (1987), the *Piper Alpha* oil rig explosion (1988), the Hillsborough football stadium disaster (1989) and the loss of the *Marchioness* on the River Thames (1989).

For those who needed justice, the fine was justice of a kind, although there was some frustration that no prosecution for manslaughter had followed. Writing in *The Times*, David McIntosh – senior partner of London solicitors Davies Arnold Cooper – pointed to the disparity between the Purley driver's imprisonment and the fact that 'no individual or corporation [could] be successfully prosecuted when inquests at public enquiries have made findings of gross and disgraceful disregard for safety'. There was, he went on, 'now widespread support for finding ways in which … corporate accountability laws [could] be improved so that available punishments [fitted] the crimes'.

As it turned out, Clapham would be a catalyst for the change McIntosh sought, in that – in 1996 – it was one of the events that led the Law Commission to make proposals which eventually led to the Corporate Manslaughter and Corporate Homicide Act.[140] Of course, 1996 was akin to 1948 in the sense that nothing had really changed on the railway – if you were travelling on an HST, it was probably still in InterCity livery, just as – if you'd been behind a 'Castle' in the first year of nationalisation – everything about the trip would have screamed 'Great Western'. The following year, 1997, was to turn out somewhat differently alas…

Lines Out of Paddington

At around 13:10 on 19 September, Larry Harrison, driver of the 10:32 from Swansea, started packing up his holdall with his diagram and notices. Rounding the curve ahead of Southall he suddenly saw a red signal ahead.[141] As the lines straightened out in front of him, he saw something else – a locomotive at what he would later describe as 'a funny angle'.[142] A collision was inevitable. He rammed on the brake. He knew there was nothing more he could do. He left his seat and hid behind the bulkhead door.

By the time he emerged again, his train would be in disarray, six people would be dead (with another soon to follow) and 139 would be injured. By seven that evening, he had been arrested.[143] By the time he had been charged with manslaughter the following April, Professor John Uff's public inquiry had begun. By the time *that* had been published,

Ladbroke Grove had occurred. This second accident took place on the morning of 5 October 1999, when a 'Turbo' bound for Bedwyn struck an inbound express from Cheltenham, having passed SN109 signal at danger.[144] Its driver, Michael Hodder, had passed a 'double yellow' and a 'single yellow' beforehand, acknowledged the AWS warning associated with them, acknowledged a third before the collision came. Thirty-one people, including both drivers, were killed; hundreds more were injured.

The inquiry into Ladbroke Grove, led by senior judge Lord Cullen, highlighted issues about post-privatisation driver training. BR's first formal course for 'footplate staff' (known as MP12) had begun in 1973; this remained in use until superseded by the modular Driver 2000 programme in 1992. In *Beyond Hidden Dangers* (2003), Stanley Hall argued that Hodder's training was only '*loosely* based on the BR system and included four weeks' traction training and 16 weeks' practical handling' (author's italics). Cullen revealed that the modified version of Driver 2000 handed over to Thames Trains in 1994 was indeed not being strictly followed by 1998. Halcrow Transmark was later commissioned to examine the situation and noted that 'signalling maps and plans [were] available for some routes but these ha[d] not been updated with essential information such as high-risk (e.g. multi-SPADed) signals, etc'.[145] Furthermore, 'route learning "norms" … d[id] not appear to recognise the risk of inexperience, particularly for newly qualified drivers with no previous operating experience over the route'.

Hodder started training on 1 February 1999; his first solo shift was on 22 September – 33 weeks later, or some 10 weeks less than the BR minimum.[146] Although his trainer had taught him that Paddington was 'tricky', and that he should count the signals from left to right to work out which one was applicable to his line, he told the inquiry he 'was not there to teach [Hodder] the routes', but 'how to drive a Turbo'. The trainer, of course, had 'grown up with the system' and had 'taken it as it … evolved'. Someone like Hodder was 'just thrown in at the deep end'.[147] Until this evidence was given, the training manager had been unaware that the trainer did not think it was part of his brief to be teaching route knowledge.

For Christian Wolmar, writing in *On the Wrong Line* six years later, the Thames training package was not so much about competence as meeting the company's need for new drivers. Former driver and safety expert Peter Van der Mark agrees, clarifying in *An Unexpected End to the Journey* (2016) that there was an 'urge to get expensive new staff out onto trains quickly in order to provide passenger miles and reduce the extremely expensive cancellations of services due to staff shortages.' Anyone who thinks cancellations are expensive, as the saying goes, should try having an accident …

Like Purley, Ladbroke Grove also highlighted issues around the sighting of signals. The approaches to Paddington had been resignalled for bi-directional working by BR in the early 1990s.[148] Many new signal heads were required, but – as space was at a premium – most were mounted on gantries. The trouble was, the curvature of the formation meant it was not always obvious to an approaching driver which one was for which line. Reflective line-identification signs had been added, but as Cullen noted, 'they were closer to the signal to the right-hand side than to the signal for the line to which they related'.[149] At the time of the accident, all the signals on the gantry that held SN109 ('Gantry 8') were at red, but the overhead line equipment for the (then) new Heathrow Express service, which had been installed with scant regard to how this would affect signal sighting, also created a situation in which the signal was the last of all those on Gantry 8 to become clearly visible (and readable) to the driver of a train approaching from Paddington.[150] Add in the low sunlight evident on the day of the accident, and one might argue that Hodder's error was inevitable.[151]

Finally, there had been a failure to learn from previous incidents.[152] If there had been a number of 'Claphams in the making' before Clapham, there were a number of potential 'Ladbroke Groves' before Ladbroke Grove. In fact, between 1 February 1993 and 2 July 1999 there had been 67 SPADs in the Paddington area, and it got worse after the overhead line equipment had been installed.[153] As Van der Mark notes, the layout 'had been conceived with the use of ATP in mind to provide collision-prevention safety'. But ATP was only fitted to Great Western HSTs and most of the SPADs involved Thames Turbos. On 10 November 1995, indeed, a Turbo passed Royal Oak's SN74 signal at danger … and struck a Great Western HST. The driver of the former had read the wrong signal on Gantry 5 that time. Only one person was injured, but the resulting report noted that 'the methods of route learning into and out of Paddington [appeared] very informal'.[154] It also noted that, of a total of 37 SPADs in the Paddington area at that point, 21 had occurred at gantries, including 12 where the driver had mistaken the correct signal.

Issues of sighting, of layout, of confusion, kept coming up. The data was there, the recommendations kept flowing, but they all seemed to fall into an administrative void. No one at Railtrack's Great Western Zone seemed to take responsibility – or be given it. Indeed – to quote Cullen – the Zone had 'no procedure for the tracking of recommendations'; there was also (perhaps more damningly) 'a culture of apathy and lack of will to follow up promised actions'.[155]

The only person who seemed to be putting all this together was Alison Forster, First Great Western's Director of Operations and Safety. Time and time again, she voiced her concern about SPADs in the Paddington area; time and time again she urged Railtrack to take action; time and time again she attended meetings where there were plenty of ideas, but no subsequent actions. She told of a lack of clarity about who at Railtrack was meant to be dealing with SPADs. She told of how – in

August 1998 – she had written to Railtrack's production manager about SN109, asking 'as a matter of urgency' what 'he intended to do about this high-risk signal'.[156] As she told the Ladbroke Grove inquiry, she 'never received a full response'. For Forster, Railtrack did not 'look very often at some of the big-picture issues'. They tended to be 'reactive to incidents'. They did not seem to be 'a learning organisation'.

Such were the similarities between Ladbroke Grove and Southall that a joint inquiry into train protection systems was launched, led by Uff and Cullen, the findings of which were published in January 2001. Protection systems had been involved in both accidents, but at Southall, Harrison's inattention coupled up with faulty AWS on the leading power car and an ATP that could not be used as Harrison was not competent to use it;[157] at Ladbroke Grove, Hodder's train would have been stopped had it been fitted – like the HST involved in that event – with ATP. Yet for Uff-Cullen, AWS *and* ATP were now 'old technology'. 'As a result of other systems now being developed,' their report went on, 'there is no longer any serious demand for general fitment of [ATP]'. One of those 'other systems' was the Train Protection and Warning System (TPWS), which had been conceived as an enhancement of AWS after cost-benefit analyses had stymied the wider installation of ATP.

TPWS was cheaper than ATP, but – like ATP – improved on AWS by automatically applying the brakes on a train that had passed a fitted signal at 'danger' or was approaching one too fast. Successful trials led to wide-scale installation from 2000. At the time, concerns mainly related to its perceived reduced effectiveness at speeds over 70mph, but though it would slow a train significantly, the system was later improved – 'TPWS+' – to incorporate additional overspeed sensors, thereby making it effective up to 100mph.

In the years ahead, TPWS would play a part in cutting the number of SPADs from around 500 a year to fewer than 300 on a railway that was steadily getting busier, and a larger part in reducing the potential consequences.[158] Yet Uff-Cullen preferred the more ATP-like European Train Control System (ETCS), which formed part of a wider European Rail Traffic Management System (ERTMS), and was designed to bring train protection homogeneity to the continent and was later embodied in European legislation. Uff-Cullen wrote that 'Having reviewed the evidence as to the current state of development of ETCS, the availability of resources and other commitments which the industry faces, we conclude that regulations should provide that all trains running at over 100mph should be protected by ETCS by the year 2010'.[159] At the time of writing this book, implementation has not progressed beyond the Thameslink Core Section, the Paddington–Reading route and the Cambrian Line.[160] At the time of Uff-Cullen, though, it was becoming clear (again) that the railway was facing other risks. Between 2000 and 2002, 21 further lives would be lost in train accidents. Ten would come on 28 February 2001, when a train struck a car that had crashed through the railway boundary,[161] but it was the derailment at Hatfield on 17 October 2000 that exposed the privatised railway's lack of safety cohesion even more starkly than Southall and Ladbroke Grove had done.

Chapter 23

Nervous breakdown

Travelling by rail hasn't been easy recently – for any of us. But now all Britain's rail companies are pulling together – doing whatever it takes to return you to a national rail network you can depend on.
National Rail television advertisement, 2001

It was the New Millennium and the feared computer blackout caused by machines flipping from 1999 to 2000 had failed to materialise. The power cuts, inconvenience and nuclear missile launches had not come and the daily grind had soon returned to the same old daily grind. It was now October, so summer was no longer singing in streets like BTF had described in *Elizabethan Express* way back in 1954. Of course, the day began ordinarily enough, just as the morning of the Clapham accident had, the morning of Purley had, of Bellgrove, Southall, Ladbroke Grove … *This* morning, the 17th, the crew that had worked empty to Skipton came back to King's Cross and took a short break. Their next train was 1D38 – the 12:10 King's Cross–Leeds – which left the capital 'right time' and snaked over the points at the station throat before entering the dark cavern of Gasworks Tunnel. Headed by 91023, followed by a retinue of Mark IV stock, it represented perhaps the last hurrah of British Rail's InterCity brand, flying now under the colours of Great North Eastern, an operator aware of, proud of, the fact that it worked 'the route of the Flying Scotsman'. Maybe 1954 was not quite so far off after all.

The speed of the thoroughbred rose as the train passed Alexandra Palace, Oakleigh Park and Hadley Wood. By 12:23, it was rounding the Welham curve at about 115mph. After passing under the Oxlease Avenue overbridge, the driver and the trainee sitting at the controls noticed that the brake pipe pressure had fallen to zero, initiating a full brake application. The reason soon became apparent – *derailment*.[162]

Though the 91 and its first two carriages stayed on the track, the remaining eight had come off. Some remained upright, others were leaning over. One – the buffet car – overturned and struck two overhead line equipment masts, both of which were brought down, both of which penetrated the carriage, one reaching down from roof to table, seat and floor.[163] It was here that the four fatalities occurred. Over 70 people were also injured, four of them seriously (including two members of staff).

The HSE closed the East Coast Main Line for three weeks to undertake a forensic fingertip search. This caused critics to compare Hatfield unfavourably to earlier accidents, when lines had been reopened quickly. Among them, Stanley Hall pointed out that the Slow lines on the four-track railway near Harrow & Wealdstone were reopened the day after the accident there in October 1952. After Colwich in 1986, the debris was removed, and the track, signalling and overhead line equipment were all restored, allowing traffic to resume after just four days.

Critics indeed thought the search added precious little to what had been learned during the first few hours, which was that the high rail of the canted curve at Welham had broken into over 300 pieces. Beyond this, the rail was intact – though displaced – for about 44 metres, though there was a further fragmented length of 54 metres beyond that. Marks on the wheels of the 91 suggested it may have passed over a fracture, after which the rail shattered beneath the first two carriages. This had already sparked concern (though perhaps panic is a better word) within Railtrack about the rail condition elsewhere on the network, sparked too the blanket imposition of a number of speed restrictions, many for 20mph, until all the facts could be ascertained. As Terry Gourvish was to write, one of 'the more controversial aspects of the activity was a decision by local Railtrack managers to close the West Coast Main Line north of Gretna on 25 October'. Sir Alastair Morton – chairman of the then <u>Strategic Rail Authority</u> – was moved to declare the whole thing a 'collective nervous breakdown'.

Ribbons of Steel

So, what had caused the high rail of the canted curve at Welham to shatter? Throughout its life, track will deteriorate with use. In *Elizabethan Express*, track maintenance gangs are shown as part of the huge team that made railways work, from the train planners to the waiters, the upholsterers to the fitters. The track gangs, *platelayers* in long-forgotten parlance, are of course the ones responsible for allowing passengers 'riding in clover' to 'take meals on velvet at 90 or over', as the film had it. Their latter-day equivalents, after the privatisation process had ended, were – as we saw – Railtrack, as infrastructure controller, but also Balfour Beatty, which had a contract with Railtrack to maintain the track, rail and signalling on the East Coast Main Line, and Jarvis Facilities, which had the contract for rail renewals.[164]

The railway's ribbons of steel suffer more when trains have wheels with flat sections, and when there is poor jointing and poor packing under the rail. This heightens fatigue, which can lead to cracks or fractures if not detected. In some cases, cracks develop deep and downward in a way that weakens the rail. Those near the gauge corner became known as 'gauge corner cracks' (GCC).[165] GCC had first been noticed in the early days of diesel traction, when heavily-laden wheelsets revolving at higher speeds were found to flake the railheads. Instances were few at first, but started to become more prevalent on the West Coast Main Line in the 1980s, partly as a result of the higher tractive efforts exerted by electric locomotives.[166] This led to a series of reports in the 1990s, started by BR and taken forward by Railtrack, which showed GCC to be playing an increasing role in broken rail incidents, the higher rail on superelevated curves being the most vulnerable, due to the higher contact stresses at the wheel-rail interface.

Though, perhaps like Clapham, perhaps like Ladbroke Grove, the accident might have seemed to come out of nowhere, in fact the Down Fast at Welham already fitted the cant and curve profile; the higher tractive effort and higher speed parts of the equation came when electrification came to the East Coast Main Line in the late 1980s. Viewed in retrospect, then, it should have been obvious that there was going to be a problem here. But though causal chains are *always* obvious when viewed from the accident back to their origin, the key players were blind to the problem, blind in part because they lacked knowledge of the permanent way they were supposed to be making sure remained permanent. There was indeed 'an incomplete appreciation of the risks presented by gauge corner cracking, and [a] consequent failure to develop and disseminate comprehensive instructions on its identification and the control measures required'.[167]

A *full* appreciation of the risks would probably have led to the rail being renewed. The last complete renewal in the Welham-Hatfield area had come under BR in 1982, using normal grade steel rail. As the decade wore on, though, so did the rail; in fact the Down Fast at Welham was found to be suffering from GCC in 1993, which is why, two years later, it was replaced with continuously welded flat-bottomed rail, which had been 'mill heat treated' in a bid to improve wear resistance in line with increasing axle loads, higher speeds and a greater traffic density.[168] Unfortunately, the fact that harder rails wear more slowly not only allows cracks to develop, it also takes longer for the rail profile to conform to the wheel profile, resulting in a smaller contact area and even higher contact stresses.[169] A problem, but less of a problem perhaps if rails are regularly checked.

Asset Integrity

There were – and are – two ways to check the integrity of a rail; by eye and by ultrasonic testing. The former was known to the gangs of the 1950s, known to the gangs of the 1850s, indeed; the latter involves the use of sound waves to check for rail flaws. It took off in 1970, when hand-held equipment was augmented by a two-car diesel unit fitted out to do the same job at 20mph. In 1977, computer analysis was added to the process, which – by the end of the century – had become a vital tool in the battle against broken rails. At Hatfield, that battle was lost, though the fight was never going to be easy, as GCC could be very hard to detect. In some respects, it was similar to a conventional internal transverse kidney-shaped fatigue crack, referred to as a '*tache ovale*' defect.[170] However, GCC differed from a 'tache ovale' in that the latter could be picked up by regular ultrasonic testing techniques, whereas GCC could propagate at a different angle, allowing it to evade the probe. To combat this, in March 1995, new testing procedures were proposed ('U14'), in which the probe was offset towards the gauge corner.[171] This allowed it to detect major fatigue cracks emanating from that corner. Once a crack was found, the U3 procedure – in which the probe is placed over the centre line of the rail – would be used to confirm it and provide an estimation of severity.[172]

Unfortunately, while the U3 examinations at Welham Green were being made at the required frequencies, the additional U14 testing using was not, meaning the full picture of the situation was blurred, meaning too that further renewal was not considered. In September 2000, though, a fourth player – SERCo Railtest – did undertake grinding in the area.[173] Grinding smooths the top of the rail, and can stop small cracks spreading further into it, but all it did in this case was smooth the gauge corner and take out all the loose chippings along the edge. This had no impact whatsoever on the effectiveness of the U3 testing, which registered 'total loss of rail bottom' and rail 'untestable' on 6 October, just as it had three times before.[174] That said, these results should have told someone that *something* wasn't right and should have stimulated a site visit by track engineers. But they didn't. In fact, as the cracks were now so deep, the grinding probably only weakened the rail even more.

Elsewhere on the network, GCC had been appearing in the causal chains of a growing number of broken rail incidents. And, to be fair, Railtrack was far from oblivious; in November 1999, it had told Balfour to list the places where GCC was present on high-speed high-canted track. Then, later that month, multiple GCC defects resulted in a serious rail break on a high rail at Aycliffe.[175] It was on the East Coast Main Line. It was another alarm bell. Balfour's list, delivered in December, identified several priority sites. Some of the worst were in the Hatfield and Welham area, and were deemed to require renewal within a month.[176] A temporary speed restriction should have been imposed at this point to ease pressure on the rail. But it wasn't. Nevertheless, the urgency of replacing the Welham curve specifically was identified the following February and scheduled for between 13 and 29 May 2000 (to be dealt with after Hatfield itself).[177] By the end of March, however, the condition of the track had deteriorated enough for this to be brought forward to the third week in April. Alas, the requisite rail was not delivered until 28 April, after three failed attempts to do so.[178] Over-running work at Hatfield caused more delay, pushing the work back until a new application was made for various dates up to 28 January 2001.

What looks now like so much incompetence or misfortune had been partly motivated by concerns about delays, which drained money from Railtrack in performance penalty costs. This is where the pre-accident reluctance to impose emergency or temporary speed restrictions also came from. The figures tell the story: on 9 October, eight days before the accident, the company had reported that, in the first half of 2000/01, delay minutes had risen 10 per cent year-on-year. This effectively wiped out the 10 per cent improvement of 1999/00 towards the Rail Regulator's 12.7 per cent target. Yet all the while the renewal was delayed, all the while the ultrasonic warnings went unheeded, the cracks continued to develop. When interviewed, the patrollers said they inspected two lines in each patrol, but their inspection reports indicated that all four lines were being inspected during one session – which of course they were.

Just as for BR with the Waterloo resignalling (though for different ideological reasons), it was a question of resourcing; at privatisation, Railtrack and its contractors had been obliged to cut costs by 3 per cent. This saw patrol teams of four or six reduced to two – a patroller and a single lookout. With just one lookout, at Welham – where trains can pass at 100mph or more – it was far too dangerous to do anything other than check the curve from the cess. One patroller said that he was able to see the high rail from this position, but only the back of the head and not the gauge corner.[179] Maybe so, but there was evidence that the deep cracks at Welham, or at least those likely to lead to failure, were linked to the localised detachment of metal from the railhead, known as surface spalling. And spalling was found to be present over a distance of at least 1,000 metres south of the derailment zone.[180] If it was a question of resourcing, though, it was also a question of training: if none of the patrollers' reports referred to fatigue phenomena like GCC, it was probably because they had not been properly trained to identify it. More worryingly, the last patroller to inspect the Welham Green curve said he had *never* been trained to recognise GCC nor understand what risks it brought with it.[181]

But of course, Hatfield wasn't just about patrols, it was about management too. Specifically, the 'track walk' inspections undertaken by Balfour's Route Section Managers (RSMs) were deficient. They were also infrequent, being well below Balfour's mandated two-monthly intervals. Another Balfour instruction stated that an RSM should ride in the cab of a train every two months to inspect conditions. Between 7 October 1997 and the day of the derailment, only eight of a possible eighteen rides had been made.[182]

The investigators also found gaps in the monitoring systems applied by those above the RSMs. On the southern section of the East Coast Main Line, the RSM track walking reports were countersigned by the Area Maintenance Engineer (AME). The AME in post between February 1999 and October 2000 had a signalling background, not a track background, which doubtless explains why he did not verify the quality of the RSM's work.[183] The AME was supported by a Regional Track Engineer, who was required to carry out a patrol every two years. He delegated the one scheduled for 2000 to the Assistant Regional Track Engineer, who completed it on 18 August, but his report made no mention of GCC on the Down Fast at Welham. He was probably just as concerned for his own safety as the patrollers, the four-second warning of approaching trains respecting neither employer nor job title. This fact, understated the HSE, 'may have resulted in a less than thorough inspection'. Indeed.

To sum up, Balfour staff at all levels had failed to follow instructions and comply with current standards. In particular, key reporting and minimum action requirements were not followed when severe GCC and spalling was detected during patrols and tests. There was also a culture of assessing GCC on the basis of visual examination alone.[184] Behind this were failures in the management of defects and a failure to provide a safe system of work to allow staff to carry out effective inspections. Such difficulties were not communicated to management, on top of which resource shortages and staff turnover resulted in the absence of knowledgeable and experienced staff to deal with rail condition issues. Indeed, there were possible training deficiencies for some of the Railtrack auditors too.[185] In interview, Railtrack's LNE Compliance and Engineering Manager said he was unable to follow a discussion about track work because he did not understand its technical nature. In interview, the Zone Quality Standards Manager said he had neither 'knowledge of railway engineering nor railway safety'. This explains why the audit process applied to Balfour was ineffective, and perhaps in particular why there was an over-emphasis on assessing documentary compliance and not the quality of the actual work. *Modern Railways* columnist Roger Ford later said that 'Railtrack got the 'B' team when it came to BR managerial talent'.[186] Readers can make up their own minds.

Familiar Lines

There are clear parallels between Hatfield and Clapham regarding staff training, supervision organisation and the financial pressures exerted by government. As with Clapham, though – as indeed with Purley, Bellgrove, Southall, Ladbroke Grove – there were front line failures and failures further up. In the case of Hatfield, the investigation found that it was not just about Balfour, or even about Balfour not acting as directed by Railtrack, but also Railtrack's failure to monitor and manage the work of Balfour effectively, and its failure to implement an effective rail renewal operation. In cases like Hatfield, there is often someone putting all the pieces together, sensing what's coming, but to no avail. For Ladbroke Grove, that person had been Alison Forster; for Hatfield, it was Professional Head of Track at Railtrack HQ, David Ventry.

In May 1999, Ventry had told senior colleagues that 'a key driver in the rise in the number of broken rails is the current poor maintenance or, more precisely, the lack of adequate and appropriate maintenance'.[187] Informed by a track walk, he wrote to his superiors in November expressing his belief that 'the current state of the track on parts of our network [was] heading towards the boundary of acceptability', clarifying on 13 November that there was 'widespread noncompliance' with track maintenance standards and good practice. More tellingly, the 'balance between commercial drivers and safety' was 'overwhelmingly towards the commercial', so much so that 'Zone Track Engineers [were] in fear of losing their jobs if they [did] not accept noncompliance'. In short, he was 'concerned that the number of broken rails and the condition of the track in some locations [was] providing an intolerable risk.'[188]

He had a point. Broken rails had been on the up since privatisation. The HSE's *Railway Safety Statistics Bulletin* had reported a 21 per cent rise, from 755 in 1997/98 to 937 in 1998/99.[189] Tom Winsor, who had become the Rail Regulator in July 1999, wrote to the company on 12 August, demanding more clarity on what it deemed acceptable. Railtrack's Safety & Standards Directorate audit report for 1999 showed that part of the problem may have been Railtrack's new 'Project Destiny' strategy.[190] Devised by management consultants McKinsey, this focused on the idea of replacing assets only when necessary and not at fixed time intervals. To take this more commercial path, one needs excellent knowledge of one's asset condition; Railtrack had no such thing. As the audit report said, the 'just-in-time approach led to major shifts from track renewals to maintenance'.

Part of the problem had been that, within Railtrack, there was no system that allowed the company to view the total number and types of rail defects affecting their infrastructure at any one time. Railtrack's Asset Database was incomplete and inaccurate, which meant it had little idea about what assets it had, their condition, and expected life expiry. Instead, it relied on information from its contractors, all of whom used different systems.

Part of the problem too was 'the depression of the professional engineering role within Railtrack HQ and LNE zone levels'. It was not just the one zone of course. It was in fact an early policy of Railtrack, under CEO (and former BR senior executive) John Edmonds, to purge 'the upper levels of the company of anyone with engineering experience' (to quote Wolmar), in the belief that outsourcing was best. This left Railtrack's engineering seam about as thin as a wet tissue on a rainy afternoon in Bognor, reducing it to the role of 'ignorant customer'. This was not going to be helpful to a 'relatively junior manager' (to quote Wolmar again) like Ventry, who had neither the authority nor the resource to bring about the improvements he felt were necessary.[191] 'It is clear,' wrote the Office of Rail Regulation (ORR), 'that he alerted senior colleagues to the non-compliant state of rail maintenance, however, Railtrack as an organisation, failed to implement and monitor his advice to ensure rails were properly maintained'.[192]

The immediate operational impact of the accident had been enormous, thanks to all those speed restrictions right across the network, and an equally massive programme of rail replacement. Performance was destroyed and costs increased substantially; between October and December 2000/01, a reported 64 per cent of trains ran on time, compared with 87 per cent during the previous quarter.[193]

The going was anything but easy for passengers, who viewed the television advertisement quoted at the top of this chapter with some suspicion at first. But though engineering was re-established as a Board level discipline and responsibility, Hatfield cost Edmonds' successor Gerald Corbett his job, Corbett having pledged after Ladbroke Grove that he would resign if there was a fatal accident found to be the responsibility of Railtrack.[194]

The financial burden (and therefore the government pressure) on the company continued to grow heavier, the post-Hatfield maintenance bill combining with the escalating cost of the concurrent West Coast Main Line upgrade and the fact that the first review of the company by the Regulator had not awarded enough money to run the business.[195] In 2001, the government grew tired of helping the company with its spiralling repair bill and, on the order of the then Transport Secretary Stephen Byers, it went into administration. By October 2002, Network Rail (effectively a not-for-dividend body created by the government) had taken over.[196] The following year, six members of staff were charged with the manslaughter of the four people killed in the accident. The charges, and similar charges against Railtrack and Balfour, were later dropped, but in September 2005, both Balfour Beatty and Network Rail (as Railtrack's successor) were found guilty of offences under the Health and Safety at Work etc Act 1974. The former was fined £3.5 million, the latter £10 million (although this was later cut by a quarter on appeal). Both were ordered to pay £300,000 in costs. The judge described their failure to abide by safety rules as 'the worst example of sustained industrial negligence in a high-risk industry I have ever seen'.

By this time, there had been another fatal accident that damaged performance and raised questions about safety and track maintenance. On 10 May 2002, a train bound for King's Lynn derailed on pointwork at Potters Bar, killing six people on board, killing a seventh struck by debris from a bridge parapet with which the rear carriage had collided. The resulting HSE report found that the points had moved under the train because the bolts that held the stretcher bars (which maintain the distance between the two point blades) had come loose or gone missing, causing them to move apart. The points had been fully inspected on 1 May by a team working for Jarvis, which had taken over the maintenance contract from Balfour in April 2001. A further visual inspection the day before the accident reported no problems. However, that evening, a station announcer heading home from Finsbury Park reported a 'rough ride' at Potters Bar after travelling over the Down Fast line.[197] A Railtrack inspection team was sent to look into it, but due to an apparent misunderstanding by King's Cross signal box staff, they were sent to the Up Fast in error.[198] Unsurprisingly, they found nothing amiss.

At first, Jarvis claimed that the poor condition of the points was down to sabotage, a stance that failed to stand up to scrutiny. Indeed, the HSE report found that other sets of points in the Potters Bar area showed similar, less-serious maintenance deficiencies, noting that the poor state of maintenance 'probably arose from a failure to understand fully the design and safety requirements'.[199] In October 2003, Jarvis announced it was pulling out of its three rail maintenance contracts. This came just a few weeks before Network Rail announced that it was taking maintenance back in-house.

Not that this was the only change in evidence. Cullen had recommended that an independent body be established to set standards (and deal with proposed changes to them), accredit product and service suppliers, establish and manage system authorities, fund and sponsor research and development, monitor safety performance, share good practice and provide safety leadership.[200] These functions were largely being addressed by Railtrack's Safety & Standards Directorate (S&SD), which also conducted formal inquiries into major accidents.

This fitted with the post-privatisation thinking of the HSE, which had concluded that the guiding mind for safety should remain within Railtrack, which at the time had been expected to remain in public ownership (it would actually be floated on the stock market on 20 May 1996). By the time the Cullen report appeared, however, John Prescott – no longer in opposition, now Deputy Prime Minister – had made the intemperate comment that he was going to 'strip Railtrack of safety', even though S&SD was independent from its parent company. Thus Railway Safety came into being, which carried on all S&SD's work, including conducting one of the inquiries into Hatfield. The work went on when the company morphed into the Rail Safety & Standards Board (RSSB) in April 2003, although the inquiries ceased when the Cullen-recommended Rail Accident Investigation Branch (RAIB) became fully operational three years later.[201]

With an irony suggesting that the lessons of Potters Bar had not been *entirely* learnt, RAIB's first major accident investigation was the Grayrigg derailment of February 2007, in which poorly maintained points felled a Euston-Glasgow Central service as it powered north. One person was killed. RAIB's report highlighted deficiencies with the inspection of the points, ringing a bell too with Hatfield, and a more distant one with the inspection deficiencies of Clapham.[202] There was also a recognisable problem in Network Rail's 'incomplete understanding of the performance of [switches and crossings]' (i.e., points).[203]

RAIB concluded that Network Rail had made only limited progress with addressing some of the more general safety engineering issues identified by the Potters Bar investigation. In particular, 'few substantive actions had been taken to [adopt] "a risk-based approach to the procurement, installation, inspection, maintenance, etc of railway points, based on an understanding of the design and safety functional requirements"'.

On the rolling stock side, the news was somewhat better. Since Ladbroke Grove, train designs had improved incrementally – as they always had done, which is why the twenty-first century built 'Pendolino' that derailed at Grayrigg performed better in that scenario than an older train would have done. As RAIB noted, the train 'avoided, almost completely, a number of hazards', its couplers generally holding the carriages together, its anti-roll bar links ensuring that most of the bogies remained attached, its bodyshell helping resist penetration. Imagine how many people would have been killed had the train been formed of a Class 50 and 14 Mark Is, as it might have been in the late 1960s. But no more: the number of Mark I carriages on the network had fallen from 2,700 in 1995 to 1,500 by 2000, with the last leaving the main line in 2005 (although South West Trains retained two Mark I units, limited to use on the Lymington branch, until 2010).

And rolling stock strength wasn't the only thing that had improved. A fully operational BRIMS had not been agreed when Railtrack took responsibility for it in April 1994, but in 1997, data collection and analysis was improved beyond measure with the development of the superior Safety Management Information System – today's 'SMIS'. The industry also improved and improved again on the way it managed the risk from fatigue. As SPAD risk was also coming down and passenger numbers were going up, maybe some sort of second Age of the Train was in the offing, a new-found new 'golden age' as the era of Clapham faded ever more into the past? Maybe. Although complacency in railways – as in anything – is never the best idea…

PART 4:

THE ELEMENTS REGROUP?

Chapter 24

Corporate Memory …

Memories are hunting horns/Whose sound dies on the wind.

Guillaume Apollinaire,
Cors de Chasse, 1912

Acalm Cardiff morning at Christmas time, 2016. A damp and misty morning, whose sun has just appeared. At Cardiff Central's Platform 7, the 08:36 to Treherbert is preparing to leave. Passengers are settling, station staff are watching, everyone is waiting. The signal clears, the doors are closed, the Right Away's received. Slowly, the unit starts to move, starts to pull out … Almost immediately, the driver realises something's wrong, realises that the points are not in the correct position. He stops the train just before reaching them.

Extensive resignalling and track remodelling work had been going on in the area since Christmas Eve and had been planned to spill over into 2017. It was the final stage of a project that had been in progress for several years, a project that involved closing Cardiff's power signal box and moving control to a new 'Wales Railway Operating Centre'. Some of the new layout had been brought into use that morning, but one set of points – 817A – had been left unsecured, undetected and set for Newport, not the Queen Street line like it should have been.

RAIB would conclude that the points had been left in this 'unsafe condition' because they had not been identified as needing to be secured by the point securing team.[204] Furthermore, no one had checked that all points needing to be secured had actually been secured. Route proving trains had also been cancelled, and a culture had developed between long standing members of the project team that led to 'insular thinking about methods of work and operational risk', meaning that team members 'relied on verbal communications and assurances'. The Branch also felt ineffective fatigue management to be a possible underlying factor behind the incident, the Senior Construction Manager having made an error while on his first night shift, having just completed seven day shifts since his previous rest day. His last two day shifts had been 12 hours long.

Simon French, RAIB's (then) Chief Inspector, drew a clear line from Cardiff back to Clapham, pointing out 'how easily things can go wrong when railway infrastructure is being upgraded and renewed,' pointing out too the importance of managing the working hours of people doing the job.[205] 'Back in 1988,' he went on, 'the disastrous collision at Clapham Junction happened in part because working for weeks on end without any days off was part of the culture in some areas of the railway'. The events at Cardiff showed 'how easy it is to forget the lessons of Clapham and slip back into those habits under the time pressures of a big commissioning'.

A few months later – on 15 August 2017 – a train departed Waterloo on a green aspect, but was incorrectly routed and collided with an engineer's train on the adjacent line. Luckily the driver saw the way the points were set and managed to brake, meaning the collision occurred at low speed and resulted in no injuries. The signalling was being altered to increase station capacity, but modification to the wiring of the point detection circuits meant that a 'desk' set up to aid testing no longer simulated the detection of the points in question correctly … because it had not been modified to take account of changes made to the detection circuit.[206] On the weekend of 12/13 August, while trains had been stopped from running on the lines leading to the points, a temporary wiring 'mod' was made in the relay room in an attempt to restore the correct operation of the relevant switch on the test desk. But the mod was not reviewed by a signalling designer and was wrongly left in place when the railway was returned to operation on the morning of the 14th.

RAIB investigated once again, its report going to some length to point out the parallels between Waterloo and Clapham – Cardiff and Clapham again too.[207] Specifically, both incidents had 'resulted from people taking actions which were inconsistent with the processes in which they had been assessed as competent. Had these processes been followed, the events would have been prevented'. RAIB found 'no evidence that the staff and organisations involved at Waterloo and Cardiff lacked a commitment to safety'. In this respect, said RAIB, 'Waterloo and Cardiff have much in common' with Hidden's Chapter 17 ('Where things went wrong – The lessons to be learned'):

> The vital importance of this concept of absolute safety was acknowledged time and again in the evidence which the Court heard. This was perfectly understandable because it is so self-evident. The problem with such expressions of concern for safety was that the remainder of the evidence demonstrated beyond dispute two things:
>
> (i) there was total sincerity on the part of all who spoke of safety in this way; but nevertheless
>
> (ii) there was failure to carry those beliefs through from thought into deed … The concern for safety was permitted to co-exist with working practices which … were positively dangerous.[208]

The next three pages of the RAIB report list all the elements of Clapham that were evident at Waterloo and Cardiff East – from the slipping of working practices to a failure to communicate up and down management lines, to a disregard for fatigue and the building of a culture of long working hours (reproduced on pages 222-5). Taken together, the bigger picture is clear, that lessons learnt in 1988 had been forgotten. The impact of the Hidden Report – though well written, though well respected – was short, and the life of the railway is long.

And that's the trouble with corporate memory; it only exists while we remember it. So, while lessons were learned in 1988, the fluid nature of the industry – in which people retire, move on, or move in from elsewhere – could not guarantee that a lesson learned 30 years ago would remain in minds 30 years on. The issue seems particularly acute on the operational side. In *Modern Railways*, Roger Ford has recorded that, when a signaller retires, for example, 'they do not just take 30-odd years of experience with them, they can take 100+ years of experience with them, as they have absorbed local knowledge from previous generations which had been passed to them'.[209] Andrew Haines, the current CEO of Network Rail, adds that, for him, the railway's 'loss of operational competence' came about after Southall, Ladbroke Grove and Hatfield, all of which led to 'a laser-like focus on asset management, consistency and compliance to make the railway safe again'.[210] Performance improvements in the years that followed came from 'improved asset reliability'; 'ops' therefore fell by the wayside.[211] The importance traditionally allotted to railway operation may also be divined from the fact that the Institution of Civil Engineers formed in 1818, the Institution of Mechanical Engineers formed in 1847, and the Institution of Railway Signal Engineers followed on in 1912. The Institution of Railway Operators was not formed until 2000, however, gaining its Royal Charter on 1 October 2021.

One must note at this point though that, for some, the 'loss of operational competence' came earlier than privatisation. In 1991, Peter

Rayner wrote a paper (*Operational Safety – A Role for the Professional*) in which he lamented the loss of such knowledge higher up in BR. Indeed, operating was 'not understood by anybody above director level and the effect of a re-organisation on that function throughout BR [was] appalling'. The effect of this on traditional operating disciplines, he went on, 'can only be guessed at, but we must all hope that the wheel turns fast enough to recover the situation whilst there is something left to recover.'[212] This was echoed in the submission made to the Hidden inquiry by Clifford Hale, via his counsel. Hale's Recommendation 3.4 is worth reproducing in full:

> It is recommended that the pro-active contribution of engineering professionalism to the effective and efficient operation of a quality railway has to be more forcefully demonstrated to, and recognised by, General/Business management. The contribution of engineers in their own disciplines, as well as being managers of others, must be more fully appreciated to ensure BR continues to attract and retain professional engineers.[213]

Yet railways are not all engineering or ops or innovation. Railways are *whole systems* – from senior managers to people insulating wires, tightening fasteners, checking, testing ... actually doing the work. Thus one could argue that privatisation exploded the railway's shared experience, its *grand narrative*, and thus the grand narrative of railway safety too, as it marched towards a world where risk, if not non-existent, was greatly reduced. Against this is the fact that some former BR men and women worked on in the Brave New World, so much so that their shared experience of, yes, Clapham, but then Southall, Ladbroke Grove and Hatfield, galvanised them to do better, to keep carrying the flower of safety forward. If one considers the downward train accident fatality trend over the last 50 years, one can argue that they were successful, but the unexpected consequence of that success is that those now joining the industry have fewer such memories to galvanise *them*.

The danger is of course that a well-meaning new broom will sweep away practices, processes and even equipment without realising why it's there and the consequences of its removal. At the same time, we need to be aware that what was a risk in 1988, 1997, 1999 may not be one in 2023 – or rather 2033, as our reliance on digital technology grows and puts a correspondingly greater emphasis on software integrity and cyber security. We do seem to keep throwing a lot of our eggs into an ever-decreasing number of digital baskets, as hitherto purely mechanical and electrical systems are replaced by those that increasingly integrate and use a wide range of additional digital technology assets and components which, together, will also change how critical functions are monitored and controlled.

In short, like aviation and maritime, rail is moving towards becoming a cyber-physical system, in which the variety of assets used, the number of stakeholders involved and the range of potential risks rises in ways which complicate our understanding of their origin, interaction, functional resilience and point of responsibility. While clearly making things like wire counts irrelevant, this cyber-physical space is not without dangers of its own, as evident from RAIB's investigation into the loss of temporary speed restrictions on the ERTMS-fitted Cambrian line (2017); the operational difficulties were evident in August 2019 when a number of Class 700 electric multiple units became stranded after a (probable) lightning strike and required a fitter with a laptop to come out and 'reboot' their systems.[214] On the Cambrian, the speed restriction data had not been uploaded during an automated computer restart the previous evening, but a display screen incorrectly showed it as being ready for transmission to trains. A way of assuring that the correct data was provided to the display had not been clearly defined in the software design documentation and the resulting software product included a single point of failure which affected both the upload and the signaller display functions. In the case of the 700s, a permanent lock-out had been designed into the software to mitigate the risk from a driver resetting the equipment when there was a safety-related fault of which they were unaware. This is an appropriate response to many scenarios, which typically impact single trains. However, the type of power supply issue that occurred that day and its potential to lock out multiple trains at the same time had not been given adequate consideration when the system was designed.

In short, it's all about understanding and managing risk. The metal fatigue cracks found on Class 385 and Class 80x series unit trains in 2021 are a reminder that, as Roger Ford put it, 'for all the talk of "digitisation", the railway remains dependent on mechanical engineering for safe and reliable operation'. Trains still run on rails and the railway does indeed need to have 'eyes everywhere'.[215] Hidden suggested BR had become almost blind to the risk from wrong-side failures in comparison to its focus on SPAD risk. BR was probably right to put proportionately more focus on SPAD risk in the late 1980s, but not to the exclusion of wrong-side failures (or any other hazard, come to that).

Of course, it's totally rational to put most risk reduction effort into the areas where risk is highest, or where there is the most scope for risk reduction ... but it is vital that risk assessments be kept fresh. On the one hand, we might consider what look like outlandish or unlikely scenarios, as these may one day catch us out. The 'Oceanic turnback' of 11 September 2001 is perhaps a case in point.[216] On this day, when a terrible attack was launched on the World Trade Center's twin towers in New York, almost 50 aircraft heading across the North Atlantic were required to return to Europe as a result of the closure of United States airspace. A contingency procedure had been developed for turning back, and some pilots initiated it. The trouble was that it had been developed for a single aircraft, not a large number of them. There were no collisions or near misses, on-board technology should have prevented that from happening anyway, but there was no strategy or means for an air traffic controller to identify which aircraft to prioritise based on position and fuel remaining.

It is also important to avoid being blinded by solid trend lines and to look sometimes at the outliers, the 'weak signals', where perhaps the data points are fewer, but where the consequences might be great if the situation is allowed to persist. There is no better argument for taking such a holistic view of risk than Clapham, preceded as it was, by a number of 'Claphams in the making', that a greater emphasis on learning from operational experience might have highlighted.

In his excellent work on 'close call' incidents, Carl Macrae makes a similar point about air accident investigators, whom, he notes, gain great 'awareness and knowledge … from being immersed, day-to-day, in the ongoing stream of incident reports'.[217] This kind of reading can sharpen one's nose for when something is not quite right. To go back further, in his autobiography, John Elliot (Chairman of the Railway Executive 1951–1953) describes a similar trait in Sir Herbert Walker, for whom Elliot had worked between 1925 and 1937. Elliot witnessed a conversation about a fatal derailment at Sevenoaks on 24 August 1927, involving a 'River' class tank engine. The designer, Richard Maunsell, told Walker that the locomotive was stable and that there must have been a problem with the track. Walker's Chief Civil Engineer said the track was in good condition. Walker replied that 'accidents do not happen by accident' and was sure the derailment had been caused by issues with both elements. As Elliot reports, Walker had been right: 'Maunsell's new tank was in fact unstable at speed on the Eastern section tracks, which were not fit for the extra weight of the heavier engines recently allocated to handle the boat trains'.[218]

In the railway industry today, incident reports are currently supplied by Network Rail. They highlight a lot of ostensibly minor events that could have been precursors to something larger, allowing rail safety practitioners to augment the trendlines derived from data by keeping a look out for things that do not look quite right.

The thing is, as Cardiff and Waterloo remind us, data and information – from the past *and* the present – are only any use if we analyse results, understand what they mean and *act* on them … out on the railway, not just on paper or a computer screen …

Chapter 25

… And How to Keep It?

Those who cannot remember the past are condemned to repeat it.
George Santayana, 1905

O ne of the most idiotic things the author has ever heard in a
railway safety meeting is 'we know all this'. The person who
said it – who happened to be chairing – should have known
better. But of course, they were thinking what many think when mid-
career, on a trajectory that's still climbing: they think they're going to
go on forever. An unhelpful assumption, of course, because it considers
today but thinks nothing of tomorrow. As for yesterday, well they were
there, so they won't forget will they?

Yesterday is important. Yesterday is the bedrock of all that comes
after. Learning, indeed, has its origins in experience, and experience
quickly becomes part of history. Here, though, one must be cautious.
Polmont happened in part because there was no precedent for it, there
having been no fatal high-speed collision in Britain involving a large-
boned animal and a push–pull train. At the same time, tests had shown
the risks to be no different from a train hauled by a heavy locomotive.
BR therefore fell foul of the law of unintended consequences. So, while
later investigators would point out that 'the passing of time without
a process accident is not necessarily an indication that all is well and
may contribute to a dangerous and growing sense of complacency',[219]
it was *after* Polmont – and not before it – that the company developed

the weightier, obstacle deflector-fitted Mark III and Mark IV driving trailers that began to appear from 1988. Similarly, the Lockington level crossing accident would lead to improvements in crossing design, while the Colwich collision led to changes in how 'flashing yellow' aspects were used at junctions.

The Lockington crossing had been changed in 1986 from one protected by barriers operated from an adjacent signal box to an automatic open crossing, remotely monitored (or AOCR).[220] AOCRs are equipped with road traffic signals and audible warnings only, operated automatically by approaching trains. Telephones are provided for the public to contact the signaller in an emergency. A safety review – led by Professor P.F. Stott of King's College, London – was published in 1987 and provided guidelines for their installation, guidelines, it noted, that 32 of the existing 44 AOCRs (including Lockington) would not meet. In these cases, the report recommended conversion to a crossing type that offered more protection. Although Stott also felt that there was 'no *prima facie* reason why [an AOCR] should not be used where they suit a special situation', in the event BR developed the automatic barrier crossing, locally monitored' (ABCL). The first ABCL to be commissioned was at Beccles, on the East Suffolk Line, in 1988. There is now only one AOCR on the network, at Rosarie in the Scottish Highlands, although (at the time of writing) moves are afoot with the local traffic authority to affect its closure.[221]

The signalling at Colwich Junction had been altered on 17 August 1986 to enable the crossover between the Down Fast and Down Slow line to be traversed at 50mph. This was achieved by introducing flashing yellow aspects at CH105 and CH103 signals. The driver of the train that passed the signal protecting the junction (CH23) at danger had wrongly believed the flashing yellows would take him all the way through that junction, even though the signal taking him through the crossover (CH28) showed a steady yellow.

Flashing yellows were first introduced for high-speed junctions only, as explained in a BTF short by John Powell, BR HQ's Traction and Train Crew Manager (cf, *Flashing Yellows*, 1978). When applied to crossovers, however, the rules were not amended, meaning that they could be interpreted incorrectly. In his RI report on Colwich, Major P M Olver said that the Rule Book was updated to make the picture clearer on 4 April 1987 but noted how 'disturbing' he found it that the original (1977) rule about flashing yellow aspects on the approaches to diverging junctions was not expanded to deal with their 'ever increasing use' on the approaches to high-speed crossovers until *after* the accident.

The need for care when changing something long established is clear. Yet it was to be the Glanrhyd Bridge collapse that would – like Clapham – be cited by RAIB as part of a lost corporate memory several years later.

Troubled Water

At 08:40 on 31 December 2015, serious subsidence occurred at Lamington Viaduct in South Lanarkshire as a passenger train passed over at over 100mph. When RAIB's report was released, Simon French drew a line from Lamington back to Glanrhyd. The investigation into the latter had found that a repair carried out to the bridge's Pier No. 2 in 1982, 'while ensuring the structural strength of the masonry of the pier, actually increased the likely damage to the pier from scouring of the foundation'.[222] French pointed out that while this had led to 'improved procedures for checking the integrity of bridges over rivers, especially at times of flood,' the causal chain of the Lamington incident was 'a reminder that, under certain circumstances, the scouring effect of a swollen river can undermine bridge piers to the point where the structure above starts to fail'.[223] The problem had been that a previous process for managing the associated risk had fallen into disuse, at least in part due to organisational change. 'The railway has seen numerous organisational changes over recent decades,' French went on. 'Although change is inevitable, and often for the better, it is vital that the railway industry finds ways to retain its corporate memory [and] associated management systems.'

When you reorganise you bleed. Fiennes saw it in the Sixties, but he was quoting his own training, which in turn was drawing on Petronius (27 AD–66 AD), who is attributed with writing that 'every time we were beginning to form up into teams, we would be reorganised. I was to learn later in life that we tend to meet any new situation by reorganising; and a wonderful method it can be for creating the illusion of progress while producing confusion, inefficiency, and demoralisation'.

This suggests that the problems of managing change are in fact archetypal to the human condition. In this book, we saw it with Clapham, we saw it with Ladbroke Grove and Hatfield. RAIB saw it with Lamington, Cardiff and Waterloo. BR learned from Polmont, from Lockington, Colwich, Glanrhyd, Clapham, Purley and Bellgrove. Lessons are easier to retain perhaps when they lead to a new piece of equipment, whose usage continues, and whose instructions are documented. But though criticised for making the railways too inward looking, and criticised by Hidden for contributing to staff losses in the mid-1980s, BR's tendency to recruit from within made it easier in some ways to pass on that flower of safety, as it meant there was always someone above who had learnt from the older railway, via long apprenticeships, mutual improvement classes and by getting their hands dirty (which would be called 'experiential learning' today). This was how the grand narrative went on. The problem comes when that narrative is disrupted: A&O III was arguably such a disruption; privatisation was arguably another.

Whatever one's political belief or point of view, the great mistake of privatisation was the barely controlled shedding of so many people with skill, knowledge, experience and understanding. The public inquiry reports reveal much evidence on this point: as we saw with Ladbroke Grove, for example, BR's driver training package had been watered down; as we saw with Hatfield, the loss of engineering capacity led to poor rail condition which led in turn to the shattering of the rail. Yet one of the myths of privatisation is that a totally new workforce suddenly came out of nowhere, when in fact many of the old BR brains carried on doing what they had always done. The problem *then* involved those above them making ill-conceived decisions. The problem *now* is that those old, experienced and knowledgeable brains are starting to retire with some rapidity. This was seen with the Lamington incident. One could also point to the case of the Malahide Viaduct in Ireland, part of which began to collapse as a train was passing over on 21 August 2009. The cause was found to be a form of water erosion known as scouring. However, in the causal chain was 'a loss of corporate memory when former Iarnród Éireann staff left the Division, which resulted in valuable information in relation to the historic scouring and maintenance not being available to the staff in place at the time of the accident'.[224]

The benefits of having a knowledgeable workforce were recognised by the philosopher Adam Smith as far back as 1776 in *Wealth of Nations*. The idea was developed further in the 1960s by two American economists, Theodore Schultz (1961) and Gary Becker (1964). By the new millennium, the European Commission was expounding the need to strive for a 'continuum' of workforce learning 'with the aim of improving knowledge, skills and competence' in order to retain a competitive edge and promote economic development.[225] As Annie Brooking also noted, 'companies rely on long-standing employees to act as their "corporate memory", but when these people leave, links to the past are permanently severed'.[226] This has concerned Stuart Webster-Spriggs, VolkerRail's Director of Safety, whose 'best fix' is to recruit people only slightly younger than retirement age – though he's aware that he'll be facing exactly the same problem in a couple of years' time. How could this be overcome? As the Chief Engineer at Siemens Mobility, Andy Stringer, notes, the task is a chimera in the extreme: 'The interesting thing about corporate memory is that we all see it from our own perspective. There is actually no such thing as corporate memory, just the collection of a group of people's own individual memories'.

This book has demonstrated two distinct corporate memory requirements: one being the need to keep remembering the lessons of Clapham while they remain relevant, the other centring on how to remember other lessons that need to be remembered. Regarding the former, and in light of the many new, young testers entering the fold, mindful too of the generation that has passed since Clapham, Neil Massey, VolkerRail's Senior Test Engineer, has produced a working simulation of the 'Clapham wiring' to demonstrate what happened on that fateful day in December 1988. Stringer gives a hard-hitting presentation to accompany his demonstration of the similar model Siemens has built. 'If every attendee gets the opportunity to be the person that moves the loose wire, that drops the relay, that clears that track, that makes the eight-year-old girl celebrate her birthday without her father,' he says, 'maybe they'll remember the errors that were made.' The author has moved the wire, and heard the chilling clunk when the relay fails to fail safe. It is a sobering moment, made more sobering still when one has the context.

It helps that the Hidden report itself is still available, nowadays free of charge on the excellent Railways Archive website, which hosts an increasing number of official accident reports all the way back to the first in 1840. In many ways, the site is the library of the railway's grand narrative, but regarding Hidden itself, the very readability of the report made it an inspiring document to anyone bent on becoming a safety practitioner.

Grand Narrative

Since 1955, Rolt's *Red for Danger* has helped the flower of safety to be carried forward. The book is, in effect, a series of narratives that forms not only the grand narrative of death by rail, but also the grand narrative of safety's evolution. At the time, *The Listener* called it an 'intensely human story' and it is this link to the human condition that makes it such an important work; when we care, we are more apt to remember. Not that Rolt resorted to gratuitous descriptions of death and devastation; nor does he put words into the mouths of those involved. So, in the story of the collision at Norton Fitzwarren in 1890, the fireman, Albert Dowling, warns his driver that there is 'a train a–coming on our line and he is never going to stop'; the signaller at Hawes Junction in 1910, Alfred Sutton, realises the full horror of his mistake and tells a driver to inform the station master that 'I am afraid I have wrecked the Scotch express'; and the driver injured at Castle Cary in 1937, D. Macaulay, when scolded for suggesting another signaller had erred, sadly shrugs 'all right, all right: there's no use getting angry about it'. All these phrases appear in the original inquiry reports. Rolt's skill is that he then adds more human colour, as in the case of Macaulay, who is described with simple tenderness as limping away after delivering his line.

Elsewhere, the language conveys fear, terror, appalling weather conditions, Rolt bringing an almost painterly eye to each scene. At the opening of his description of the double collision at Abbots Ripton in January 1876, for instance, the reader is asked to 'imagine a heavy coal train of thirty-seven wagons rumbling slowly southwards from Peterborough'. In its cab, driver and fireman peer for signals 'through puckered eyes round the cab side sheets for the spectacle glasses were blinded with snow'. You can hear the rhythm of the wagons on the track joints, feel the white-cold of the whiteout as the engine's fire roars in the firebox… As *The Times* wrote in its own review, 'Many who repeat glibly the claim that British railways are the safest in the world have no real idea on what basis this claim is made'. *Red for Danger* helped explain that claim, Rolt noting that Abbots Ripton had been caused in part by a signal freezing in the clear position, despite the signaller setting it to danger to protect a train on the line ahead. A couple of pages later, he explains how the accident therefore led to changes and improvements in signalling such that henceforth signals were held at danger until cleared for a specific train to pass (although today of course the multiple aspect preference is invariably to keep signals clear unless protecting the section ahead).

Examples like this may be found throughout the book, making its grand narrative a teleological one, aiming for an ultimate end – though far more than Rolt could have realised. Rolt updated his work in 1966, but died in 1974. The statistics since then reveal passenger fatalities in train accidents (collisions, derailments, etc) to fall away to zero until Grayrigg in 2007 and then zero again until 2020, when a driver, guard and passenger were killed when a train struck a landslip at Carmont on 12 August. This reminds us that if the circumstances are right – or wrong – the links in a causal chain can still join to form an accident, no matter how good modern systems, equipment and people are. Furthermore, as the Lamington Viaduct incident reminds us, our assets have long lives; even the Class 88 locomotives which are relatively new at the time of writing could still be on the network for another 40 years.

The past may be a foreign country, but in railways not *everything* is done differently there.

Knowledge Management

Storytelling, though stretching right back to the oral tradition, is now vaunted anew as a means of managing knowledge, generating emotional connections, keeping the corporate memory alive. Stories stick, their lessons stick, and they are more easily remembered when they need to be. All this is why *Red for Danger* remains vital. We should all make time to read more anyway, about everything, but a recommendation to read *Red for Danger* is no guarantee that a new starter in rail will do so. This realisation that it was no longer 1955, when a large part of the railway's intake was related to someone already on the job, began in the late 1980s as we saw. In 1955, new starters were also more likely to be interested in railways before they joined, and would need little encouragement to read around the subject. The classic British enthusiasm for rail still exists, but the vein pumps less strongly than it did, meaning that the level of understanding is less too, and *Red for Danger* does assume quite a lot of prior knowledge on the part of the reader. As Andy Stringer points out, even if 'staff are sent on training courses, books are recommended, students are told to go research or read up on what happened', it can have 'much the same impact as doing nothing, although it does leave you with the warm feeling of having done something and the illusion that the corporate memory is now the same as your own'. Although books can inspire people, and people can change companies, books do not change anything by themselves. Neither do films, nor even wiring models. So what *else* can be done?

In Japan, a possible solution has presented itself in the form of the East Japan Railway Company's Accident History Exhibition Hall.

Opened at the company's General Education Center in 2002, it features video footage of past accidents, reports and documents, but also full-size replicas of trains and actual vehicles that have been involved in major incidents. The idea is to encourage staff to implement safe behaviour 'through a combination of theoretical training and practical learning about the history of [its] safety systems, the process by which [its] operating rules were decided, [its] attitude toward accident prevention, [and] the importance of protecting the lives of passengers and other people'.[227] In October 2018, the facility was enhanced by the opening of an Interactive Learning Hall. Here, rolling stock that was involved in a derailment at Kawasaki in 2014 is preserved. The new hall's purpose is 'to encourage reflection on derailment accidents from various perspectives'. By exhibiting the vehicles involved in the accident, along with digital signage, actual records from the time, and so forth, says JR East, 'we are providing a deeper understanding of the nature of the job and past accidents and pursuing training that will enable personnel to put safe behaviour into practice'.

In Britain, RSSB produces 'a number of learning presentations and documents relating to the relevance of corporate memory to railway safety'. This includes 'articles in Rail Safety Review, a publication available to RSSB members'.[228] The Learning from Operational Experience Annual Report (produced until 2017) also captured information learnt in the given year, often tying it back to lessons learnt in the past. In addition, RSSB has produced an animated presentation on Ladbroke Grove, while Network Rail and RSSB contributed to *Learning from History*, a document dealing with corporate memory and published by *Rail* magazine, which referred (*inter alia*) to the lessons from Clapham.[229]

Several of the old BTF films have been referred to throughout this book. The unit was established in May 1949, soon after nationalisation, and went on to produce many award-winning features, including one (*Wild Wings*, 1965) which won an Oscar for 'Best Live Action Short'. Yet it wasn't all travelogues and modernisation reports. Some, like *Mishap* (1958) and *Emergency* (1962) advised staff on what to do if an incident occurred, while *The Finishing Line* (1976) and *Robbie* (1979) warned schoolchildren on the perils of trespass and, in the case of the former, vandalism. Films like these, and *Safety Knows No Boundaries* (1981), do not bolster the corporate memory *per se*, although *Train Time* (1952) showed the effort taken to cope with operational problems – from the Station Master in Cornwall getting on the phone to Marazion for more wagons to carry broccoli up to London, to the difficulties of planning a new freight that does not get in the way of passenger services. Swap the tweeds, the pipes and fountain pens, and modern rail staff would recognise many of the issues – and many of the workarounds – today.

BTF shorts were shown to schools and clubs, but also at cinemas ahead of the main feature. Here, it would help inform the audience of the day about what it was like to work on the railways, and what was involved. Its drip drip of information would get through, would make important books like *Red for Danger* easier to understand, make that delay on the 8:15 easier to understand too.

Today, RAIB is helping to preserve the corporate memory visually by commissioning an animated reconstruction of the fatal tram derailment that occurred at Sandilands on 9 November 2016, while RSSB produced an episode in its 'RED' staff briefing series (49, *Past at Danger*), which strove to chart the history of SPAD events and their mitigations.[230] Yet it is Network Rail, through its own film unit, which is carrying the BTF torch forward, using digital technology and social media platforms to reach out to a wide audience with films like *The Railway at War: 1935-1945*, which was released in 2020 to mark the 75th anniversary of the end of the conflict, and uses the company's Safety Central website as a platform for its accident reconstruction and analysis shorts.[231]

These are very much the macro-scale, full industry versions of a solution, although all rely on collaboration, on people 'being bothered' to read or watch or listen. On the micro scale, storytelling and those with a longer history in the industry are absolutely vital. For one thing, not all new ideas are good, and not all old ideas are bad (and vice versa), but it is not a case of getting the retiring railway person to 'download their brains' – an oft-used, and thoroughly villainous, dehumanising phrase. And while JR East, experiencing a similar 'rapid change in the generations of its employees, including frontline staff' has 'assigned ex-employees …who possess an abundance of knowledge and applied skills in railway safety to act as … "Chroniclers of Safety"', it's not necessarily a case for formalised procedure.[232] As Michael Woods, former BR Dartford Area Manager and later Principal Operational Specialist at RSSB, explained: 'sometimes I don't know what I can remember until I remember it; it's the conversations about safety that help bring this detail or that back to the front of my mind.' Most time-served railway staff are only too pleased to have these conversations. Steve White, Managing Director of Southeastern, recalls that – at London Underground – lunchtime talks were regularly held 'to explain the causes of and lessons from previous incidents'. It was valuable 'for colleagues of all ages and experience'. Sometimes, though, the pride of youth means that youth will not ask questions of the old; and sometimes the old are too cynical about the willingness and ability of youth to understand. Sometimes the young are too quick to seek experience for their CVs before they move on to other jobs, and other industries, thus failing to accumulate knowledge and failing to appreciate why what they did in their last position might not be relevant, useful or safe in rail. Sometimes the old forget that the railway has moved on from 'their day' and sometimes the young think they know it all. Sometimes indeed the young prefer short films or podcasts, and the old want shorter and shorter reports, both missing the detail that can be so vital to safety. The best situation is somewhere in between all this, with both sides reading, talking – and *listening* – more.

If the lessons of Clapham are to survive, and if (more generally) the corporate memory is to survive, such that the railway retains *all* the lessons, *all* the nuggets, *all* the proverbial 'good stuff' it has learned in the past – we're going to have to keep telling the stories. Whether this be embodied in training, in procedures, in formalised briefings or less formal discussion, the human element will remain. Technology will doubtless help in a big way. Technology will doubtless improve our various databases, digital resources and risk analysis tools. But none of it will be much good if we don't talk about the lessons and keep on sharing them. After all, we do *not* 'know all this'. No one ever has, or ever will.

Chapter 26

Afterword

Only connect.

E. M. Forster,
Howards End, 1910

This chapter offers a summary of the main points we've learned so far.

Thinking of Clapham specifically, one must note first that no one person was to blame. The accident was caused by a series of errors, misjudgements and failings that happened to combine in a particular way on 12 December 1988 with particularly tragic consequences. So, the front line made a human mistake that supervision and management did not pick up on (pages 60-5; 72-5). Management also missed the weak signals from reports of similar wrong-side failures, partly because it did not have the systems to be able to do so, partly because its sights were set on what it perceived to be the bigger problem of SPADs (page 116). If there is to be *one* lesson from Clapham, then, it's that safety is not all about trendlines, that much vital information will be 'buried' in the daily incident reports and that it is therefore important to have eyes everywhere (pages 112-8). It is also important to remember that just because all appears to be well, that does not mean it *is*. As James Reason wrote, 'the large random component in accident causation means that "safe" organisations can still have bad accidents, and "unsafe" organisations can escape them for long periods. Bad luck can bring down the deserving, while good luck can protect the unworthy.'[233]

Aside from the high fatality count, one of the reasons Clapham continues to stand out more than, say, Polmont is that it was the subject of only the third public inquiry in the (main line) rail industry's history, thereby putting it into the same canon as the Tay Bridge disaster of 1879 and the Hixon level crossing collision of 1968 (page 68). It also came at a time when thinking about safety was changing, in light of a number of non-rail accidents, including the Bradford City fire (1985), the sinking of the *Herald of Free Enterprise* (1987), the King's Cross Underground fire (1987), the *Piper Alpha* oil rig explosion (1988), the Hillsborough football stadium disaster (1989) and the loss of the *Marchioness* on the River Thames (1989) (page 152). Any sense of complacency about safety could not be allowed to remain in this context.

Hidden would give Clapham longevity by shining a light not only on the accident itself, but also the organisational structure of BR. But one must not get carried away with the notion that everything was rotten in the state of S&T and nowhere else. Rather, S&T may be considered a microcosm of BR's troubles at that time. Indeed, Peter Rayner made the point that S&T was 'unlucky' with Clapham, 'because [such an accident] was [in fact] more likely to have happened to the Operating function, which had many more less technically trained staff at risk'.[234] To illustrate the point, he described an incident from 1989 in which a motor alternator fell from a carriage and derailed a train near Harrow. The alternator had come off due to the progressive failure of its securing bolts. When Rayner, as Regional Operations Manager of the London Midland Region, investigated, he found that:

> in pursuit of business goals to drive InterCity into profit in response to government spending targets, costs had to be

reduced. Engineering standards were to play second fiddle to bottom line accountability and in consequence, the interval between inspections of the motor alternator securing bolts had been significantly extended.

When he questioned a Mechanical & Electrical Engineering witness as to why the interval had been extended, the answer was '"cost–effective maintenance"'.[235]

The cultural issues evident in the Clapham causal chain were also evident beyond BR. The Fennell report on the King's Cross fire, for example, also pointed (*inter alia*) to cultural deficiencies at London Underground, which had been 'struggling to shake off the rather blinkered approach which had characterised its earlier history', which was 'in the middle of [...] a change of culture and style', and yet accepted that 'fires were inevitable on [what was] the oldest and most extensive underground system in the world'.[236]

Back to the subject of cuts, another lesson from Clapham is that if you have not got the staff, you won't be able to complete your project to plan, if that plan was formed when you had more staff. And if you are losing staff, it is likely to be down to something in the wider world, which affects rail far more than its huge literature usually suggests. In the case of BR in the 1980s, the organisation could not recruit and keep sufficient workers because of working conditions, yes, but also because of money. BR's staff wanted more money and often sought it in other industries. Money was also the reason why it took so long to get WARS through BR's own approval process, why BR had 'sectorised' at the start of the decade, and why it brought in A&O III halfway through it (pages 93-105). Nowadays, A&O III might well be cited as a causal factor in the Clapham accident, but the financial context explains the need for it: BR did not have much money to start with, but the government wanted to give it less. Yet the government wanted to give it less largely because of the prevalent politico-economic conditions of the time, coupled perhaps with concern about BR's ability to manage major projects, like the APT. Some mandarins may even have remembered the diesel locomotive over-ordering in the 1950s and viewed the railway of the late 1980s accordingly (pages 95 and 122). The irony is that while governments often want to cut railway funding, they seldom appreciate the wider contribution railways make to the economy, such as getting people into and out of London, for example. The Covid-19 pandemic of 2020-21, in which the railways got key workers and vital supplies where they needed to be when they needed to be there, may have taught those in power something on this point. Then again, it might not.

As we have recalled several times, Gerry Fiennes said 'when you reorganise, you bleed'. However, if we substitute 'reorganise' for 'change', we can throw the net more widely. Clapham was a case of change upon change, in terms not only of reorganisation but also resignalling at the same time, yet Morpeth, Polmont, Lockington, Colwich, Glanrhyd, Purley and Bellgrove can all come in here too. On the surface of it, they were all very different. Dig a little deeper, though, and the linking theme becomes more apparent:

- **Morpeth** occurred in part because the fitment of AWS to the Down line after a similar accident in 1969 was not extended to the Up line, as it failed to meet the fitment criteria for doing so, featuring a 'cascade' of descending speed restrictions, rather than a single one, as on the Down (pages 33-4).
- **Polmont** came in part from the introduction of new push-pull driving trailers which were light enough to be felled by a large-boned animal in a certain position on the line – demonstrating perhaps that

Reason's 'trajectory of opportunity' can get through no matter how small the holes in some of the cheese slices may be (pages 30–3).

- **Lockington** came in part from the introduction of a new type of open crossing that could be misused or used erroneously by road drivers (pages 34; 86).
- **Colwich** involved the introduction of new flashing yellow aspect signals at junctions without first ensuring that drivers understood what they meant from a SPAD risk point of view. Interestingly, the Stedeford Group's proposals led to the cancellation of some smaller electrification schemes, and a scheme to build a flyover at Colwich, whose presence would have negated the circumstance that led to the accident (pages 34; 86–7).
- **Glanrhyd** involved a repair to a bridge pier which increased the susceptibility of that pier to scour at the foundation (pages 34–5).
- **Purley** resulted in part from a resignalling such that signal sighting was impaired (pages 69; 112–14).
- **Bellgrove** came from the introduction of cheaper single lead junctions that could put trains on a collision course if a SPAD occurred (page 113).

Later years would highlight problems of amending training packages, adding overhead line equipment without considering how this affects signal sighting (Ladbroke Grove, pages 153–8) and changing rail maintenance procedures without fully considering derailment risk (Hatfield, pages 159–73). The *reasons* for these changes are another matter, of course. At Ladbroke Grove, the change to driver training was down to a post-privatisation 'urge to get expensive new staff out onto trains quickly in order to provide passenger miles and reduce the extremely expensive cancellations of services due to staff shortages' (page 155). At Hatfield, the desire to minimise costly delays put performance before track maintenance (pages 168-9). As Hatfield showed in particular, privatisation led to the loss of experienced railway brains, in the belief that a filing cabinet full of contracts was better than a knowledgeable management team (page 169). Privatisation, in terms of both changes to structure and changes to ownership, also created a vacuum in the sense that there was no obvious leadership, no company loyalties and multiple aspirations. The loyalties that *did* exist were to the industry ('the railways'), to the skill (signalling, driving and so on) or to the trades unions. Esprit de corps and corporate memory were arguably the two biggest losses during those years.[237]

Not that privatisation was solely behind Ladbroke Grove and Hatfield. For Peter Rayner:

> The matrix organisation [at BR] of business-controlled finance and function-controlled operations was a difficult matrix indeed, and it had caused the application of minimum standards in some places. The matrix had been moved by Organising for Quality from the top of the system, where it had made life difficult for managers and accountants, to the bottom of the system, where it made life more difficult for the staff.[238]

This, for Rayner, also made 'safety more complex to manage'.[239] Privatisation put some emphasis on money, but we know that money had been an issue for decades. Yes, there were external forces which forced (or guided) the governmental hand (pages 98-102), but governments did have a choice about where cuts were made, and as the second Bob Reid pointed out, 'the railways [had] always been tail-end Charlie' when it came to funding (page 149).

We have already seen how the outside world can impact on the railway – from the oil crisis of 1973 (page 99), to public sector pay strikes in 1979 (page 100) to changes in the wants and needs of staff in 1987/88 (page 108) and power outages in 2019 (page 181). These links continue. On 10 April 2021, an empty HST derailed on a crossover at Dalwhinnie, thanks to a wiring error made when a point machine was replaced. The maintenance team did not notice the discrepancy, but RAIB also found that the maintenance tester had suffered from Covid-19. He later started to experience general tiredness, memory loss and concentration issues. He did not tell his manager, as he thought he was coping and that his tiredness was the result of other wellbeing concerns that his manager *did* know about. RAIB was 'unable to completely discount' any problems the tester started to have as a result of Covid-19.[240] The long-term effects of Covid are yet to be fully understood, but it is clear that it will impact on the fatigue question the railway has been trying to answer since Clapham. It is also clear that wiring errors can still be made, and still not be spotted, in 2021.[241]

The point is that almost any change, to technology, processes, rules and personnel, will affect risk. Marianna White, RSSB's Key Engagement Manager, sees the ebbing tide of corporate knowledge, recognizes the dichotomy at play and the dangers it brings: 'The railway needs to make changes, evolve, take on new ideas and learn from other industries,' she explains. 'BUT it is essential that knowledge and experience is harnessed to ensure they are not lost ... the risk is too great'.

It is impossible to disagree, and it's all about balance. We all must change and adapt to new phenomena. But change is when we need the lessons of the past the most, and many changes are made by "new brooms" (page 91). Hence new brooms should talk to the older ones, both remembering that not all old ideas are bad and not all new ideas are good (and vice versa).

New brooms should talk to those who sweep the front line and listen to what they have to say. Safety is about people as well as processes and paper.[242] Yet new brooms should not surround themselves with people just like them. If they do, they may simply reinforce their own view of the world, and not challenge themselves. A BBC documentary has suggested that this may have been evident in the 'Ripper Squad' of the 1970s/80s, which was made up – it recounted – of white, middle-aged, middle-class men. Whether they were or (as the documentary posits) were not able to see Peter Sutcliffe's crimes from a woman's point of view, the suggestion that they may have had distinct, entrenched and self-perpetuated ideas about his female victims is a lesson worth carrying forward. In short, diversity of thought and perspective can broaden one's social understanding – a useful tool when trying to ascertain why people do what they do, whether committing a crime or making an error that leads to an accident.[243] Shortfalls in this breadth can be met by reading more widely. This includes novels, which are about people, and can help broaden one's understanding of motives, passions, drivers and so on. Actually talking to people should not be underestimated either…

Diversity in all senses is vital, but so is humility, so new brooms should also remain grounded and avoid making change that demonstrates simply that they have made "a difference"; safety is a commitment, not a career stepping stone. New brooms (at all levels) should consider the lessons of the past before repeating mistakes made before those lessons were learned; and they should, if change is deemed The Answer, at least make it as human a process as possible, encouraging people to come *with* them. Do not do change *to* anyone. That's the A&O III way, the privatisation way too. And we know what happened there. Ultimately, it all boils down to this:

New brooms: look before you sweep.

Postscript

As this book was being finalised, RAIB's report into a train accident near Carmont in August 2020 was published. A passenger service had derailed, having struck a landslip and a bridge parapet before some of the vehicles fell down an embankment. The driver, guard and a passenger were tragically killed. It was the first fatal train accident since 2007 (pages 172-3). RAIB's investigation noted that the landslip had been caused by heavy rainfall, which has been linked to climate change – a change of a different type, and which presents perhaps an even bigger challenge to the industry than the current change to digital technology (pages 181-2). Yet Carmont also highlighted issues around a more familiar sort of change.

In 2009, Carillion Construction Ltd was commissioned by Network Rail to design and build cutting slope remedial works, including a drainage system, for the deep cutting next to the accident site.[244] Unfortunately, 'Network Rail's construction assurance processes,' reported RAIB, 'were intended to operate in the context of the framework agreement between Network Rail and Carillion which required Carillion to be responsible for self-certifying construction work. Quality and inspection records [were] not available as a result of Carillion entering liquidation in 2018'.[245]

There is a parallel with the loss of documents pertaining to the Lamington Viaduct scour incident, which revealed that a 'Flood Action procedure was originally in the Network Rail Safety Manual with other procedures which were not part of the Operations Manual'. However, the Safety Manual 'was withdrawn sometime after 2004'. There was no overarching extreme weather plan document 'so the procedures were held as a series of standalone documents, lacking any formal document control or audit arrangements'. RAIB was informed that there were approximately 65 control instructions which were not included in the audit process.[246]

More recently, RAIB reported on a derailment at Watford North in September 2016, caused when a train struck a landslip. In this case, the contractors working on the cutting slope made serious errors because 'The site had not been identified by Network Rail as being at risk of a flooding-induced landslip. Such a landslip had occurred at the same location in 1940, also causing a derailment. Drawings from the 1940s relating to a structure subsequently constructed to repair the slope were held in a Network Rail archive but were not available to either Network Rail's asset management team or the designers of a slope protection project which was ongoing at this location at the time of the accident. As a consequence, this project made no provision for drainage.'[247]

Of course, it's not just railways, and the author was told of similar issues in the financial services industry. One business discarded documents believed to be outdated. It lost much valuable non-digitised information in the process. Part of the problem was that staff members in certain locations had no knowledge of what the documents were, and their importance to the business. More irritatingly, perhaps, there was a procedure specifying which particular documents needed to be kept, but not describing how to identify them. Some were saved by the older members of the business, who knew what they were looking at and were able to take appropriate action.

The rail industry is awaiting the next phase of the Williams-Shapps plan to create a new body, 'Great British Railways', originally intended to be a state-owned public company to take over from Network Rail as infrastructure manager, and also control the contracting of train operations, timetabling, the setting of fares and the collection of fare revenue. There is a concern that paperwork may be lost, but it's about much more than that. Writing in July 2021, Roger Ford made the point that – at the time of privatisation (page 167) – 'Railtrack got the 'B' team when it came to BR managerial talent'.[248] Richard Clarke, an ex-BR signaller who became a trainer in the early 1990s, agrees that the privatisation process led to a situation where 'experienced railwaymen were deserting the sinking ship, frustrated at seeing all the disasters unfolding before their eyes'.

For Clarke, among the worst elements of the (old) new world were 'the lack of checks and balances within permanent way departments [meaning that contractors and sub-contractors] with little railway experience' could find themselves on the line, perhaps having 'swapped their weekend duties with a friend' or brought their safety certificate on the black market.[249]

For Ford, this changed when 'a hardcore of old-BR operators was lured back to run Network Rail'. But as he says, what happens now? Will this new reorganisation cause the new railway to bleed? Volker's Stuart Webster-Spriggs reiterated after the announcement that 'there is an exceptionally high number of people in our industry now with less than a year's service, so have no idea about Hatfield, Clapham and so on'. The older ones could mentor them, and one would like to think this would be useful (page 190). But what if many are tempted to take redundancy or severance payments, in light of the Williams–Shapps push to change the culture, of its need to 'include meaningful numbers of people in management and senior management roles with substantial experience outside Network Rail, including in some cases from outside the rail and transport industry altogether'?[250]

RSSB is trying to aid the situation – backed by the Department for Transport – by producing a guidance document, detailing some of the lessons of the past, the pitfalls that can arise when organisations are changed and how they might be avoided. The author has a small hand in this project, which – it is hoped – can be imbedded in the industry's future thinking and be drawn upon to keep the corporate memory alive. Will it work?

It would be easy to write 'Who knows…?' and leave it at that – especially as a new Prime Minister reshuffled Shapps away from transport in 2022, meaning that – in February 2023, at least – the big change to Great British Railways looked itself set to change. But if this book shows anything, it shows that the more we change, the more we do need to read, listen and learn from the experiences of those who came before us.

The 35 who lost their lives in the Clapham accident

Gillian ALLEN

Clive William ATTFIELD

Jane Melanie AUBIN

John Felmingham BARRETT

James Robert BEASANT

Michelle BOYCE

Timothy Charles BURGESS

Glenn Ashley Allen CLARK

Arthur George CREECH

Norman Edward DALRYMPLE

Brian Richard Gerald DENNISON

Stephen Michael DYER

Romano FALCINI

Paul Derek George HADFIELD

Edna Rosa HANNIBAL

Geoffrey Ralph HARTWELL

Stephen Griffiths HOPKINS

Everett William Parks LINDSAY

Stephen John LOADER

Joseph MARTIN

Alison McGREGOR

Christopher Roger MOLESWORTH

David John MOORE

Teresa MOORE

Michael NEWMAN

Beverlie NIVEN

Austin Paul PERRY-LEWIS

Alan PHILIPSON

John Philip ROLLS

Alma SMITH

Tracey STEVENS

Erroll Derek TAYLOR

David Arthur George THOMAS

William Joseph WEBB

Alan WREN

Glossary

4–REP	'4–REP' refers to an electric multiple unit (qv) of **4** vehicles, with **R**estaurant car and **E**lectro-**P**neumatic braking; each four-car set included two 1,600–hp motor coaches.
adapted diesel–electric	In the context of Chapter 2, this refers to the 98 1,550–hp diesel-electric locomotives built by the Birmingham Railway Carriage & Wagon Works (BRCW). They had been specifically designed for the Southern Region. The first (D6500) was delivered on 4 December 1959. Between 1965 and 1967, 19 were fitted with the necessary equipment for the Bournemouth-Weymouth push-pull operations.
Advanced Passenger Train (APT)	The APT was developed by BR engineers brought in from the aerospace industry. It featured an 'active tilt' system that allowed it to minimise passenger discomfort at up to 155mph by leaning into curves. The early experimental gas turbine train (APT-E) was later replaced by an electrically powered prototype (APT-P), intended to work the West Coast Main Line.
approach locking	The purpose of approach locking is to prevent the change of route ahead of a signal once the driver has seen a proceed aspect at the signal or has seen an aspect at a previous signal indicating that the former signal is displaying a proceed aspect.
automatic half–barrier (level) crossing (AHB)	Automatic half-barrier crossings are equipped with barriers that only extend across the nearside of the road (so that the exit is clear if the barriers start to lower when a vehicle is on the interface). The barriers are activated automatically by approaching trains and rise again when the train has passed, unless another one is approaching.

Automatic Warning System (AWS)	AWS uses a permanent magnet in the track to trigger a warning, unless it is followed immediately by an electromagnet that provides the opposite polarity magnetic field – in which case a 'clear' indication is given. As designed, AWS will sound a 'bell' in the cab whenever the signal ahead of the magnet is green, and a 'horn' ahead of any other aspect. If a restrictive aspect is encountered, the brakes are automatically applied unless the driver acknowledges a warning within the allowed time period; a 'sunflower' reminder indication is then displayed in the driving cab. Once applied, the emergency brakes bring the train to a stand. AWS is normally positioned 180 metres on the approach to signals, thus giving the driver a few seconds to view the signal if their attention has been elsewhere. AWS does not physically prevent a train from passing a signal at danger. It was later adapted for use with permanent and temporary speed restrictions.
Automatic Train Protection (ATP)	ATP automatically restricts the speed of a train on the approach to a signal at danger. With ATP, a driver is still required to observe signals, but is given a target speed indication associated with the speedometer. An audible warning is given if the limit is infringed; if the driver then fails to reduce speed appropriately, the system applies the brakes.
'bell and black disc'	This is the AWS (qv) indication for a clear signal. A horn sound and a so–called 'sunflower' indication denote a restrictive aspect (ie, a 'double yellow', 'yellow' or 'red').
British Railways	The Transport Act of 1947, brought in by Clement Attlee's Labour administration (1945-51), saw the Great Western, London Midland & Scottish, London & North Eastern and Southern railways (along with fifty smaller companies) taken into public ownership from 1 January 1948. It also created a British Transport Commission, which oversaw Executives that initially ran bus companies, road hauliers, docks, hotels, canals, tramways, shipping lines, London Transport and (from 1949) British Transport Films. The trading name of the Railway Executive was British Railways, which – from January 1965 – was shortened to British Rail.

Cess	The area either side of the railway immediately off the ballast shoulder. It usually provides a safe area for authorised persons to stand when trains approach.
Class 27	This refers to the 69 1,250-hp diesel–electric locomotives built by the Birmingham Railway Carriage & Wagon Works (BRCW), similar in design to those it had built for the Southern Region (see 'adapted diesel–electric', above). The first Class 27 was delivered in June 1961, the last appeared in October 1962. The 12 locomotives that retained their steam heating boilers were designated Class 27/1s; the 12 fitted with electric train heating became Class 27/2s.
cost per equiv-alent fatality avoided	An economic value used to quantify the benefit of avoiding a fatality (by the adoption of some new policy or technology, and so on).
crashworthiness	The ability of a structure to protect its occupants in the event of a crash.
cyber-physical system (CPS)	Cyber-Physical Systems (CPS) comprise interacting digital, analogue, physical, and human components engineered for integrated functionality. Cyber systems can be open to malicious attack, meaning that ticketing systems, on-board wi-fi functions, signalling, etc could all be open to attack, just as the WannaCry cyber-attacks in 2017, confirmed by the UK National Cyber Security Centre as a state-sponsored North Korean initiated attack, caused significant disruption to the German rail network.
detonator	A detonator is a small round device, which is placed on the top of the rail (usually secured with two lead straps). It explodes as a train passes over, thereby emitting a warning to the driver.
diesel multiple unit	A diesel multiple unit (usually abbreviated to 'DMU') is a self-contained train powered by on-board diesel engines.
'driving brake second open' (DBSO)	Later redubbed a 'driving brake standard open', these vehicles were essentially an air-conditioned Mark II brake carriage with a cab installed at the guard's van end.

electric multiple unit	An electric multiple unit ('EMU') works on the same principle as its diesel counterpart (see above), using electric traction motors in place of the diesel engines.
English Electric Type 3	English Electric Type 3 No.6700 (later 'Class 37') was converted for push-pull testing by the Railway Technical Centre at Derby. The trials involving the locomotive were successful, but its class was deemed unsuitable for the Edinburgh-Glasgow services as (at the time) there was no facility for installing electric train heat. There was also some doubt about their suitability for sustained high-speed operations.
European Rail Traffic Management System (ERTMS)	ERTMS is a Europe-led system to facilitate, improve and develop international rail transport services within the European Union. It includes the adoption of the European Train Control System (ETCS), which uses on-board and trackside equipment to provide protection via in-cab signalling through continuous track to train data transmission.
multi-aspect colour light signals	Four-aspect signals use combinations of four lights. From the top of the signal head to the bottom, the lights are yellow, green, yellow, and red. A 'red' means that the next section contains a train. A single yellow (using the lower yellow) means that the next section is clear but there is a train in the one after that. A 'double yellow' means that the next two sections are clear. A 'green' indicates that the next three sections are clear. Three-aspect signals work in similar fashion, but without the 'double yellow' indication.
'pacific' locomotive	This term is used to denote a steam locomotive with a 4-6-2 wheel arrangement (being a four-wheeled bogie at the front, six powered, coupled driving wheels, and a two-wheeled pony truck at the cab end). During Oliver Vaughan Snell Bulleid's tenure as Chief Mechanical Engineer of the Southern Railway, two 'Pacific' classes were produced. The first 'Merchant Navy' appeared in 1941. They were among the first locomotives to use welding in the construction process and featured a thermic siphon in the firebox (a large tube which allowed water to be heated more quickly and improved boiler circulation). A lighter variant, the 'West Country' / 'Battle of Britain' class, followed in 1945.

Radio Electronic Token Block (RETB)	RETB centralised signalling in one control centre, using radio communication between that centre and the locomotive cab, thereby allowing all other signal boxes on a given route to close.
Rail Regulator	The Rail Regulator was a statutory office, created with effect from 1 December 1993 by section 1 of the Railways Act 1993, for the independent economic regulation of the British railway industry. The office was abolished from 4 July 2004, using powers under the Railways and Transport Safety Act 2003, when (in line with constitutional changes made to other economic regulatory authorities) the single-person regulator model was replaced by a nine-member corporate board called the Office of Rail Regulation – the ORR, which now has certain roadway responsibilities, hence its latest moniker, the Office of Rail and Road.
readability (of signal)	This refers to the ability to interpret a signal and its meaning correctly.
Railway Operating Centre (ROC)	A 'railway operating centre', or ROC, is a twenty-first century innovation from which the signalling equipment over a wider area than hitherto possible can be controlled.
'right away'	The term 'right away' refers to the completion of station duties, meaning that a train may depart.
Safety Risk Model (SRM)	This considers hazardous events (that is, those that could lead to harm). Each event is broken down into the precursors that could lead to its occurrence. The risk associated with each hazardous event and its precursors is estimated, and the results presented numerically.
section	This is usually used to refer to a length of running line between two absolute block sections, that is between the last stop signal controlled by one signal box and the home signal controlled by the next one. Under multi-aspect signalling, it can be used to denote the length of line between signals.

Sectorisation	In terms of British Rail, this was the division of the organisation into five different business 'sectors', each with their own bottom line. The original sectors were: InterCity, London & South East (later Network SouthEast), Railfreight, Provincial (later Regional Railways) and Parcels. 'Sub-sectors' were later brought in based on commodities carried (eg, Railfreight Petroleum) or lines of route (eg InterCity Cross Country).
Solid State Interlocking (SSI)	The brand of the first-generation processor-based signal interlocking system. It was developed by British Rail, GEC and Westinghouse.
SPAD	This stands for 'signal passed at danger'.
'sparks effect'	'Sparks effect' refers to the increase in patronage often seen when a line is electrified. It may be explained by a number of factors. For one, electric trains are seen as more modern and attractive to travel on, offer a faster and smoother ride and often go hand in hand with a general infrastructure upgrade. For another, the increased speed and acceleration of electric trains often increases capacity, meaning more trains and therefore a better service for passengers.
Strategic Rail Authority (SRA)	The Strategic Rail Authority (SRA) was established under the Transport Act 2000 to provide strategic direction for the rail industry. Abolition came with the Railways (Abolition of the Strategic Rail Authority) Order 2006, the SRA's functions being absorbed by the Department of Transport or ORR.
superelevated curves	This is the amount by which the outer edge of a curve on a railway line is banked above the inner edge. This banking allows a train to traverse the curve at a faster speed than would be safe (or comfortable) if the curve was flat or level.

(Thames) 'Turbo'	This refers to the Class 165 diesel multiple unit. Initially known as 'Networkers' or 'Networker Turbos', they were built at BR's York Works from 1990 to 1992 originally for Network SouthEast.
Time Division Multiplex (TDM)	A method of transmitting and receiving a number of data channels over a single pair of wires. The technology can be used in signalling, but also the control of locomotives, as used on the Scottish Region of British Rail to control push-pull trains featuring Class 47 locomotives, initially between Glasgow and Edinburgh.
track circuit / track circuit clip	A track circuit is a simple electrical device. Sections of line are insulated from each other, and a low-voltage current is passed along one rail of a section and back along the other. When the current is flowing, the switch in the associated relay is kept closed. A train in the section will short-circuit the flow, open the switch and return the signal behind the train to danger. A track circuit clip is a length of wire connecting two metal spring clips which can be attached to both rails. It does the same job of short-circuiting the flow and can therefore be used to protect a line by ensuring the signal for that section returns to danger.
trailing crossover	A connection between two lines of railway, by which a train travelling in one direction can reverse over to the opposite line when required.
Train Protection and Warning System (TPWS)	TPWS utilises pairs of loops placed 50–450 metres on the approach side of a signal. The loops are energised when the signal is at danger. The distance between the individual loops (the arming and trigger) determines the minimum speed at which the on-board equipment will apply a train's emergency brake. When a train's TPWS receiver passes over the first loop, a timer begins to count down. If the second loop is passed before the timer has reached zero, the TPWS will activate.

undetected	'Undetected' means that the position of a set of points is not linked to the signalling system or interlocking. This means that there is the potential for conflicting routes to be set across the points unless appropriate mitigation measures, such as securing the points in a known and agreed position, are taken.
wrong-side failure	A wrong-side failure describes a failure condition in a piece of signalling equipment that results in an unsafe state. In the case of Clapham, this meant a signal showing a "false clear", ie, green when it should have been red.

Hidden Report recommendations discussed in this book

Recommendation	Text
1	BR shall ensure that there is rigorous implementation of the practice of cutting back redundant wires, insulating, and securing them, so that there is no risk of wires coming into contact with working circuitry. Cutting back must be done before commissioning.
3	BR shall enforce tighter control on Design Office procedures for the production, issue and amendment of documents to ensure that all working drawings are complete and are an accurate representation of the system to be worked on and of the work to be done to that system.
9	BR shall introduce a national testing instruction with all speed. Such introduction shall be accompanied by a full explanation to the workforce, including workshops or seminars as necessary. Implementation must be monitored and audited.
12	BR shall ensure that there are effective systems for distributing Departmental Instructions on a personal basis to all relevant employees and that provision is made for the situation where an employee moves to a new post.
13	BR shall ensure, as a matter of practice, that all staff understand and regularly re-read the Departmental Instructions relevant to their posts. In addition, every two years, those staff involved in an annual appraisal interview, shall sign a statement to the effect that such Instructions have been recently read and understood.

Recommendation	Text
14	BR shall give technical training as necessary to ensure that efficient and safe practices are carried out by all technical staff.
15	BR shall provide refresher courses for installers at intervals of not more than five years.
16	BR shall urgently progress and monitor training and certification of testers. Refresher courses shall be evolved.
17	BR shall ensure that the structure and content of courses are regularly reviewed.
18	BR shall ensure that overtime is monitored so that no individual is working excessive levels of overtime.
20	BR shall monitor and forecast wastage and recruitment of skilled S&T staff and take urgent steps to ensure that sufficient numbers of skilled staff are retained and recruited to match work requirements safely.
25	BR shall introduce, within S&T Departments, a system of reporting and reviewing all WSFs and shall ensure that they are classified according to potential for danger, and that they are monitored up to and including Board level.
36	BR shall continue to press ahead with its Total Quality Management Initiative and the application of British Standard BS5750: Quality systems.
38	The Court endorses the use of outside consultants to review safety management issues within BR and recommends that the consultants proceed with their programme with the greatest urgency looking particularly at problems of communication up and down the organization.
40	BR shall give a higher priority to the introduction of on-train data recorders to assist investigation of any future incident.

Recommendation	Text
43	BR shall implement as a priority its programme to install a system of radio communication between driver and signaller on all traction units. The introduction of this system shall be in addition to signal-post telephones and not automatically entail their removal.
46	The Court welcomes BR's commitment to introduce Automatic Train Protection on a large percentage of its network, but is concerned at the timetable proposed. After the specific type of ATP system has been selected, ATP shall be fully implemented within 5 years, with a high priority given to densely trafficked lines.
48	The Department of Transport and BRB shall make a thorough study of appraisal procedure for safety elements of investment proposals so that the cost-effectiveness of safe operation of the railway occupies its proper place in a business-led operation.
51	BR shall ensure that during driver training the definition of a signalling irregularity and situations which are reportable are given greater emphasis.
52	BR shall ensure that drivers, reporting on signalling irregularities, are given appropriate feedback on the outcome.
59	Government shall seek to amend S.41 of the Road and Rail Traffic Act 1933 to clarify what work has to be approved by the Secretary of State after inspection, if necessary, and to include rolling stock within the terms of the statute.

Table 2 from RAIB's report on the Waterloo incident (reproduced with permission)

This table appeared in RAIB's report on the collision at Waterloo discussed in Chapter 24. It compares the shortcomings at Clapham, Waterloo and Cardiff East.

Clapham 1988	Waterloo 2017	Cardiff East 2016
Working practices were permitted to slip to unacceptable and dangerous standards.	Documented processes for controlling design modifications and testing were not used when uncontrolled wiring was installed.	The project team had developed a work group culture that led to insular thinking about methods of work and operational risk.
Full documentation was not available.	Out of date maintenance drawings in the relay room were not identified as superseded.	Individual signalling stage scheme plans had not been produced for the sub-stages of the stage 5 works. If such plans had been available, it would have been clear which points required securing. There was no single project document with a complete list of all the points that required securing.
The quality of testing did not meet standards set by BR.	The testing led changeover process was not followed. Test logs were not raised, during previous stages of the project, for test desk wiring omitted from the interlocking design drawings. Information for a reliable wire count	The tester in charge signed a form confirming that he had received confirmation that all out of use points were safely secured and padlocked. The points were not listed individually, and the tester in charge signed the form on the basis that the senior construction manager had confirmed that the points had been secured. This was non-compliant with the standards

Table 2 from RAIB's report on the Waterloo incident   223

Clapham 1988	Waterloo 2017	Cardiff East 2016
	was not available as the spur wires were not recorded on the interlocking detailed design documents (not a cause of the accident).	governing the commissioning of signalling equipment because the senior construction manager was involved in carrying out the work.
There was no effective control over the Design Office to ensure that the workforce were supplied with drawings which accurately reflected the work to be done.	The effect of the interlocking design changes on the test desk was not apparent because the spur wires (temporary works) were not recorded on the interlocking detailed design documents.	There was no single project document with a complete list of all the points that required securing. Individual signalling stage scheme plans had not been produced for the sub-stages of the stage 5 works.
Failure to communicate effectively both up and down the lines of management.	OSL testers were aware, shortly before commissioning, that the test desk might not function correctly, but the necessary management actions were not communicated to relevant staff.	The all-team briefing contained a considerable amount of information, much of which was superfluous to many of the attendees. People who attended the briefing said that they had difficulty filtering out the information that was relevant to them as there was so much detail, even where they were familiar with the whole scope of works.
	No one was allocated the task of securing points outside the blockade although this task was listed in the test plan and discussed at a risk workshop.	The designated project engineer (a senior member of staff) had removed the responsibility for checking the securing of points from the tester in charge, as he believed the tester in charge had too much else to do. However, the designated project engineer did not allocate the responsibility to anyone else.

Hidden report	Applicability to Waterloo	Applicability to Cardiff East
Hidden Recommendation 3 BR shall enforce tighter control on Design Office procedures for the production, issue and amendment of documents to ensure that all working drawings are complete and are an accurate representation of the system to be worked on and of the work to be done to that system. [The implementation of this recommendation resulted in the development and publication of the signalling design handbook.]	Compliance with the signalling design handbook would have resulted in the test desk spur wires being shown on the interlocking detailed design documents. It is probable that this would have led to recognition that the test desk needed updating.	Compliance with the signalling design handbook would have resulted in a stage scheme plan being produced. This should have shown all of the redundant points which should have been secured.
Hidden Recommendation 4 BR shall urgently ensure that an independent wire count is carried out as a matter of practice during testing. It shall be the responsibility of the person in overall charge of testing to ensure and to document that an independent wire count has been done. This function may be delegated to works staff who did not do the work. [An expectation that workforce includes management is apparent in paragraph 17.11 of the Hidden report: 'the errors go much higher and wider in the organisation than merely to remain at the hands of those working that day'.]	The drawings for the modified interlocking at Waterloo did not show the test desk spur wires and so did not show the information needed to implement this recommendation reliably. No wire count was undertaken (or required) before the possession was handed back before the accident so this is not a cause of the accident.	

Table 2 from RAIB's report on the Waterloo incident   225

Hidden report	Applicability to Waterloo	Applicability to Cardiff East
Hidden Recommendation 9 BR shall introduce a national testing instruction with all speed. Such instruction shall be accompanied by a full explanation to the workforce including workshops or seminars as necessary. Implementation must be monitored and audited. [The implementation of this recommendation resulted in the signalling works testing standard.]	Compliance with the signalling works testing standard would have provided the controls needed to prevent installation of the uncontrolled wiring. Monitoring and auditing of the workforce should have been sufficient to recognise that attitudes had changed by 2017 to the extent that some signalling staff no longer saw the need for strict compliance with process, or the reasons for doing so. Explanations to the workforce limited to technical issues would not be expected to achieve this.	The tester in charge signed a test certificate (the master test certificate) to confirm that all out of use points were safely secured and padlocked. The tester in charge had received confirmation that the points were secured from the senior construction manager. However, this had not been independently verified as required by the signalling works testing standard. This finding at Cardiff East supports the conclusion in the adjacent column concerning monitoring and auditing.
Hidden recommendations 18 and 19 BR shall ensure that overtime is monitored so that no individual is working excessive levels of overtime. BR, in conjunction with the Unions, shall introduce the concept of scheduled hours within the Signals and Telecommunications Department in order to make better provision for work which has to be carried out at weekends.		The project team had signed up to a fatigue management agreement but it was not reliably implemented. The investigation found evidence of a widespread disregard of the agreed rules on hours of work and a culture of working long hours.

Table of Causes

The table below lists some of the causal factors behind the accidents discussed or referred to in this book.

Date	Location / name	Industry	Fatals	Causal factors
30/07/84	Polmont	Rail	13	Boundary management Inadequate response to reports received (vandalism) Inadequate rules (reporting of animals on the line) Inadequate appreciation of risk Management of change (rolling stock, operation thereof)
11/05/85	Bradford City football stadium	Civil	56	Fire (dropped cigarette onto flammable debris) Inadequate appreciation of risk Financial pressures (re stadium renewal)
26/07/86	Lockington	Rail	9	Level crossing user error Inadequate appreciation of risk Management of change (level crossing type)
19/09/86	Colwich	Rail	1	Front line error (signal passed at danger) Inadequate rules (unclear) Management of change (rules and signalling)

Date	Location / name	Industry	Fatals	Causal factors
06/03/87	Herald of Free Enterprise	Maritime	193	Front line error (failure to close bow doors) Inadequate supervision Poor communications Poor safety culture Staff fatigue
19/10/87	Glanrhyd	Rail	4	Flooding Inadequate appreciation of risk Management of change (repair to bridge pier)
18/11/87	King's Cross	Rail / Underground	31	User error (smoking on Underground despite ban) Fire (dropped match onto wooden escalator /flammable debris) Inadequate maintenance Poor safety culture Poor organisational culture Poor communications Inadequate appreciation of risk
06/07/88	Piper Alpha	Oil	167	Management of change (platform design) Complacency (safety culture) Poor communications Placing of personal safety over process safety

Date	Location / name	Industry	Fatals	Causal factors
12/12/88	Clapham	Rail	35	Front line error (wiring) Inadequate supervision Inadequate training Inadequate resourcing (government pressure, world issues) Inadequate planning Fatigue (staff) Management of change (signalling, organisation) Inadequate response to previous incidents Failure to recognise weak signals Poor safety culture
04/03/89	Purley	Rail	5	Front line error (failure to heed in-cab warnings) Inadequate response to previous incidents Management of change (signalling) Presence of Mark I type coaching stock
06/03/89	Bellgrove	Rail	2	Front line error (failure to heed in-cab warnings) Management of change (track layout) Inadequate resourcing (requiring cheaper track layout) Presence of Mark I type coaching stock
15/04/89	Hillsborough	Civil	97	Crowding (inadequate control of) Inadequate response to previous incidents Inadequate response to reports received Inadequate resourcing Inadequate (pre-match) planning Management of change (terrace design and capacity)

Date	Location / name	Industry	Fatals	Causal factors
20/08/89	Marchioness	Inland water	51	Front line error (poor lookout on both vessels involved in collision) Inadequate supervision and management Inadequate competence management Possible staff fatigue issues Failure to respond to previous incidents Inadequate government regulation Management of change (conversion of vessel and visibility from control position)
08/01/91	Cannon Street	Rail	2	Front line error (failure to brake) Possible intoxication Inadequate supervision Lack of train protection system on terminal road Presence of Mark I type coaching stock
15/10/94	Cowden	Rail	5	Front line error (signal passed at danger) Distraction (guard in cab) Presence of Mark I type coaching stock
19/09/97	Southall	Rail	7	Front line error (signal passed at danger) Distraction (driver packing bag) Non-functioning train protection system (AWS) Inadequate maintenance Inadequate safety culture Management of change (introduction of regulation policy to minimise train delay without risk assessment) Appreciation of risk

Date	Location / name	Industry	Fatals	Causal factors
05/10/99	Ladbroke Grove	Rail	31	Front line error (signal passed at danger) Inadequate training Inadequate resourcing Management of change (signalling, resourcing, training) Inadequate response to reports received Inadequate safety culture Inadequate appreciation of risk
17/10/00	Hatfield	Rail	4	Inadequate training Inadequate resourcing Staff and management expertise Inadequate asset management Inadequate asset knowledge (technical) Management of change (organisation) Inadequate response to reports received
28/02/01	Great Heck	Rail	10	Road vehicle incursion Fatigue (road vehicle driver)
10/05/02	Potters Bar	Rail	7	Inadequate maintenance Inadequate training Inadequate response to reports received Inadequate asset knowledge (technical) Inadequate asset management
23/02/07	Grayrigg	Rail	1	Points failure Inadequate asset management Inadequate asset knowledge (technical) Management of change (timetable and impact on inspections) Inadequate maintenance inspection Inadequate supervision

Date	Location / name	Industry	Fatals	Causal factors
21/08/09	Malahide	Rail	0	Inadequate inspection Inadequate training Inadequate response to reports received Inadequate asset management Inadequate asset knowledge Loss of corporate memory
31/12/15	Lamington	Rail	0	Inadequate appreciation of risk Inadequate inspections Inadequate communication Inadequate resourcing, leading to: Management of change (organisation), leading to: Loss of corporate memory
29/12/16	Cardiff East	Rail	0	Management of change (signalling) Inadequate safety culture Staff fatigue Loss of corporate memory
15/08/17	Waterloo	Rail	0	Management of change (signalling) Inadequate competence management Loss of corporate memory
12/08/20	Carmont	Rail	3	Asset management Management of change (climate) Loss of corporate memory (documentation)

To underline the above, that is 18 counts of change management across all the accidents listed – twice the number of front line errors.

Select Bibliography

Space precludes referencing all the books and articles used in connection with this book, but some of the key texts are listed below.

Reports, etc

BRITISH RAIL, Management Brief 32/88, 21 December 1988

BRITISH RAILWAYS BOARD, *CLAPHAM JUNCTION RAILWAY ACCIDENT: The Implementation of the Recommendations of Sir Anthony Hidden QC* 19 February 1990

---, *CLAPHAM JUNCTION RAILWAY ACCIDENT: The Implementation of the Recommendations of Sir Anthony Hidden QC, Second Progress Report* 20 August 1990

---, *CLAPHAM JUNCTION RAILWAY ACCIDENT: The Implementation of the Recommendations of Sir Anthony Hidden QC, Third Progress Report* 21 February 1991

---, *MANAGEMENT BRIEF: Committee on the Review of Railway Finances, 2/83* BRB, 20 January 1983

---, *Oxted: Signalling failures following commissioning, 6103/7891m* BRB, 7 January 1986

---, *PRESS RELEASE: Good Progress Made on Clapham Accident Safety Measures, BR Tells Government,* 14/90, 19 February 1990

---, *SPECIAL REPORT: Report of a Joint Inquiry held from Wednesday 14 December to Tuesday 20 December 1988 at Waterloo into the circumstances of a collision between Earlsfield and Clapham Junction* BRB, 1988

CULLEN, William, The Rt Hon Lord, *The Ladbroke Grove Rail Inquiry, Part 1 Report* (London: Health & Safety Commission, 2001)

---, *The Ladbroke Grove Rail Inquiry, Part 2 Report* (London: Health & Safety Commission, 2001)

CULLEN, William, The Rt Hon Lord and Professor John Uff, QC FREng, *The Joint Inquiry into Train Protection Systems* (London: Health & Safety Commission, 2001)

OFFICE OF RAIL REGULATION, *Train Derailment at Hatfield: A Final Report by the Independent Investigation Board* (London: ORR, July 2006)

RAIL ACCIDENT INVESTIGATION BRANCH, *RAIL ACCIDENT REPORT: Serious irregularity at Cardiff East Junction, 29 December 2016* (Derby: RAIB, 2017)

---, *Collision at Waterloo, 15 August 2017* (Derby: RAIB, 2018)

---, *Loss of safety critical signalling data on the Cambrian Coast line, 20 October 2017* (Derby: RAIB, 2019)

---, *Derailment of a passenger train at Carmont, Aberdeenshire, 12 August 2020* (Derby: RAIB, 2022)

RAILWAY SAFETY, *Formal Inquiry – Final Report: Derailment of Passenger Train 1D38 1210 King's Cross to Leeds between Welham Green and Hatfield on 17 October 2000* (London: Railway Safety, 2001)

UFF, Professor John, QC FREng, *The Southall Rail Accident Inquiry Report* (London: Health & Safety Commission, 2000)

Parliamentary, etc

HANSARD, various

WILLIAMS, Keith, *Great British Railways: The Williams-Shapps Plan for Rail* (London: HMSO, 2021)

Newspapers and journals

DACRE, Marcus, 'Effective systems? Working for National Air Traffic Services during 9/11', *Rail Safety Review 56* (London: RSSB, September 2021)

REASON, James, 'The Contribution of Latent Human Failures to the Breakdown of Complex Systems', *Philosophical Transactions of the Royal Society of London. Series B, Biological Sciences*, 12 April 1990, 327 (1241): 475–484

STREETER, Tony, 'The last "proper" 100…by a doomed locomotive', *Steam Railway* (April 29–May 26 2011), p.78
Modern Railways, *Rail*, *Rail Enthusiast*, *The Times*, various issues

Books

CLOUGH, David N., *APT: The Untold Story* (Addlestone: Ian Allan Publishing Ltd., 2016)

ELLIOT, Sir John, *On and Off the Rails* (London: George Allen & Unwin Ltd., 1982)

FIENNES, Gerard, *I Tried to Run a Railway*, 2nd edn (Shepperton: Ian Allan Ltd., 1973)

GOURVISH, T. R., *British Rail 1948-73: A Business History* (Cambridge: Cambridge University Press, 1986)

---, *British Rail 1974-97: From Integration to Privatisation* (Oxford: Oxford University Press, 2002)

---, *Britain's Railways 1997-2005: Labour's Strategic Experiment* (Oxford: Oxford University Press, 2008)

HALL, Stanley, *Hidden Dangers: Railway Safety in the Era of Privatisation* (Shepperton: Ian Allan Publishing, 1999)

---, *Beyond Hidden Dangers: Railway Safety into the 21st Century* (Hersham: Ian Allan Publishing, 2003)

MUIR, George, *Bob Reid's Railway Revolution* (London: Unicorn Publishing Group, 2021)

PARKER, Sir Peter, *For Starters: The Business of Life* (London: Jonathan Cape Ltd., 1989)

RAYNER, Peter, *On and Off the Rails* (Stratford-upon-Avon: Novelangle Ltd., 1997)

ROLT, L. T. C., *Red for Danger*, 2nd edn (London: Pan Books Ltd., 1960)

VAN DER MARK, Peter, *An Unexpected End to the Journey: An Introduction to International Accidents On and Around Railways* (Shrewsbury: Shrewdale Publishing, 2016)

WOLMAR, Christian, *On the Wrong Line: How Ideology and Incompetence Wrecked Britain's Railways* (London: Aurum Press Ltd., 2005)

Notes

1. Cited in Hansard, BRITISH TRANSPORT COMMISSION (Advisory Group). HC Deb 13 April 1960, vol. 621, cc.1343-402, 1367.
2. Michael Baker, *The Waterloo to Weymouth Line* (Wellingborough: Patrick Stephens Ltd., 1987), p.26.
3. John Betjeman, *London's Historic Railway Stations* (London: John Murray (Publishers) Ltd., 1972), pp.74-75 (and ibid).
4. British Rail, *The National Traction Plan: Diesel and Electric Locomotives, Revised* (BR: London, December 1968), p.9.
5. British Railways Board, *Report and Accounts 1976* (London: BRB, 1977), p.7.
6. Department of Transport, *RAILWAY ACCIDENT: Report on the Derailment that occurred on 30th July 1984 near Polmont in the Scottish Region, British Railways* (HMSO: London, 1985).
7. Department of Transport, *RAILWAY ACCIDENT: Report on the Collision that occurred on 19th September 1986 near Colwich Junction in the London Midland Region of British Railways* (London: HMSO, 1988), p. 5 (para 7).
8. Gerard Fiennes, *I Tried to Run a Railway*, 2nd edn (Shepperton: Ian Allan Ltd., 1973), p.126.
9. Chris Green, 'One railway for London', *Modern Railways* (October 2012), pp.68-73, p.70.
10. Department of Transport, *Investigation into the Clapham Junction Railway Accident, Anthony Hidden QC* (London: HMSO, 1989) – hereafter 'Hidden' where cited – p.23, para 3.3. Note: the Hidden report refers to Haywood as 'Hayward'.
11. British Railways Board, *SPECIAL REPORT: Report of a Joint Inquiry held from Wednesday 14 December to Tuesday 20 December 1988*

at Waterloo into the circumstances of a collision between Earlsfield and Clapham Junction (London: BRB, 1988) – hereafter 'BRB Clapham'– p.5, para. 3.2.5.1 (and ibid).

12. BRB Clapham, p.5, para.3.2.5.1; Hidden, p.24, para.3.8; p.27, paras. 4.1-4.3.
13. Hidden, p.28, paras. 4.12-4.13.
14. There is a disparity in the reports on the time of Pike's train. The BRB report has it as the 06:35; Hidden has it as 06:53. The timetable confirms Hidden's version to be a typo.
15. Hidden, p.31, para. 4.28.
16. This occurred at 13:04. Ibid, p.37, para. 5.29.
17. Network Rail *Facing Points* podcast: 'The Clapham Junction Rail Disaster', interview with Gordon Pettitt, conducted by Kevin Martin (09/09/22).
18. George Muir, *Bob Reid's Railway Revolution* (London: Unicorn Publishing Group, 2021) p.273.
19. British Rail Management Brief 32/88, 21 December 1988, pp.1-2 (and ibid).
20. Department of Transport, *Railway Safety: Report on the safety record of the railways in Great Britain during 1988* (London: HMSO, 1989), p.v., para 1.
21. British Rail Management Brief 32/88, p.2.
22. BRB Clapham, p.1, paras. 1.2-1.3.
23. Ibid, p.3, para. 3.1.
24. Ibid, p.3, para. 3.1.3.
25. Ibid, p.3, para. 3.1; para. 3.1.4.
26. Ibid, p.11, para. 4.3.1; p.3, paras. 3.1.5-3.1.6; Hidden, p.61, para.7.27.
27. Under SL-53, Bumstead did not have responsibilities for testing, as an addendum to the BRB report dated 3 February 1989 pointed out. BRB Clapham, p.16, para. 4.3.8.7; p.24, para. 5.3 (and ibid); p.17, para. 4.3.8.9.
28. BRB Clapham, p.3, para. 3.1.7; p.15, paras. 4.3.6.2-4.3.6.3.
29. Ibid, p.3, para. 3.1.9; p.13, para. 4.3.3.2.4; Hidden, p.62, para. 7.37; p.9, para. 1.16.

30. BRB Clapham, p.3, paras. 3.3.1–3.3.4 (and ibid); Hidden, p.50, para.6.14.

31. BRB Clapham, p.23, para. 4.10.2; Appendix R.

32. BRB Clapham, p.9, para. 3.3.4; Hidden, p.52, para.6.21-6.28.

33. BRB Clapham, p.10, para. 4.1.1.

34. Ibid.

35. Ibid, p.10, para.4.1.2 (and ibid).

36. Ibid, p.10, para.4.2.1.

37. Ibid, p.10, para.4.1.3.

38. Ibid, pp.10-11, para.4.2.4-4.2.9; p.11, para. 4.3.2.1 (a).

39. Ibid, p.12, para. 4.3.2.1 (b); ibid, para. 4.3.2.2.

40. Ibid, para. 4.3.3.

41. Ibid, p.13, para. 4.3.3.2.1; para. 4.3.3.2.5.

42. Regarding SL–53, the 'S' denoted signalling, the 'L' testing and commissioning specifically.

43. BRB Clapham, p.14, para. 4.3.4.5; p.16, paras. 4.3.8.1.–4.3.8.4.

44. Issue 1 of SI–16 was dated 18 November 1983; Issue 1 of SL–53 was dated 3 April 1987. Ibid, p.14, para.4.3.4.3-4.3.4.7. Hidden would later report that the first time Hemingway actually saw SI–16 was at the BR joint enquiry in December 1988. Hidden, p.101, para.11.15.

45. BRB Clapham, p.19, paras. 4.5.1-4.5.4.

46. Ibid, p.14, para.4.3.4.7.

47. Ibid, p.16, para. 4.3.7.6; p.15, para. 4.3.7.1-4.3.7.2.

48. Ibid, p.16, para. 4.3.7.4.

49. Ibid, p.24, para.5.6.

50. Hansard, Railway Accident (Clapham Junction), HC Deb 12 December 1988, vol. 143, cc.647-655, 647. In terms of the legislation for ordering a public inquiry, the 1871 Act was superseded by the Inquiries Act 2005.

51. Hansard, Railway Accident (Clapham Junction), 654-655.

52. Stanley Hall, *Hidden Dangers: Railway Safety in the Era of Privatisation* (Shepperton: Ian Allan Publishing, 1999), p.24.

53. Hidden used the term 'wiring error'. Hidden, p.53, para.6.27.

54. BRB Clapham, p.18, para.4.3.11.1; Hidden, p.66, para.8.9.

55. RSSB, RS/504 Issue 1, *Managing Fatigue – A good practice guide* (London: RSSB, September 2012), para.2.1, p.12.
56. BRB Clapham, p.15, para. 4.3.7.3.
57. Ibid, p.16, para.4.3.7.4.
58. Ibid, addendum, 3 February 1989 (extra paragraph numbered 4.3.10.6).
59. British Railways Board, *Oxted: Signalling failures following commissioning, 6103/7891m* (London: BRB, 7 January 1986), p.1 (and ibid). Hereafter BRB Oxted.
60. Ibid, p.2 (and ibid).
61. Ibid, Appendix A (and ibid).
62. Ibid, p.3 (and ibid).
63. Hidden, p.85, para. 9.50.
64. BRB Oxted, p.4 (and ibid).
65. Ibid, p.5 (and ibid).
66. Ibid, p.6 (and ibid).
67. Hidden, p.87, paras. 9.59-9.61 (and ibid).
68. Ibid, p.86, para.9.52; Appendix H ('Figures produced by BR on wrong-side failures prior to the [Clapham] accident'), p.201.
69. Peter Rayner, *On and Off the Rails* (Stratford-upon-Avon: Novelangle Ltd., 1997), pp.325-326.
70. Hansard, Railway Accident (Clapham Junction), HC Deb 12 December 1988, vol. 143, cc.647-655, 649.
71. This was commissioned in February 1984. BRB Clapham, p.10, para.4.1.2.
72. David Brandon and Martin Upham, *Ernest Marples: The Shadow Behind Beeching* (Barnsley: Pen and Sword Books Ltd, 2022), p.67; p.116, ibid and passim.
73. Hansard, British Transport Commission, HC Deb 10 March 1960, vol. 619, cc.642-652, 643.
74. Hansard, British Railways, HC Deb 26 October 1960, vol. 627, cc.2358-2495, 2358.
75. The Transport Act 1968, Part IV, Section 39, para. 1, p.58.

76. Gourvish 2, p.103; Department of Transport, *RAILWAY FINANCES: Report of a Committee chaired by Sir David Serpell KCB CMG OBE* (London: HMSO, 1983), p.15, para. 2.19.

77. Serpell, p.32, para.6.25.

78. Report by Johnathan Maitland in his report for BBC Radio 4's *Today* programme, 13 December 1988.

79. Department of Transport, *RAILWAY ACCIDENT: Report on the Collision that occurred on 4th March 1989 at Purley in the Southern Region of British Railways* (London: HMSO, 1989), p.28, para. 4.3; Department of Transport, *RAILWAY ACCIDENT: Report on the Collision that at Bellgrove Junction on 6th March 1989* (London: HMSO, 1990), p.19, para.147; p.9, para.64; Rayner, p.11. See also Health & Safety Executive, *A report of an Inquiry into the collision that occurred on 21 July 1991 at Newton Junction* (London: HMSO, 1992).

80. Department of Transport, *Bellgrove*, p. 4, para.25; Hall, *Hidden Dangers*, pp.57-58.

81. Department of Transport, *RAILWAY ACCIDENT: Report on the Collision that occurred on 19th December 1978 between Hassocks and Preston Park in the Southern Region of British Railways* (London: HMSO, 1980), p.14, para.47.

82. Ibid, para.48.

83. Ibid, para.49.

84. Ibid, para. 50.

85. Ministry of Transport, *RAILWAY ACCIDENTS: Report on the Double Collision which occurred on 8th October 1952 at Harrow & Wealdstone station in the London Midland Region of British Railways* (London: HMSO, 1953), p.27, para.104.

86. Hidden had also referred to the "distorting beam" of hindsight early on. Hidden, p.3, para.16.

87. BRB Clapham, p.15, para. 4.3.7.3.

88. David N. Clough, *APT: The Untold Story* (Addlestone: Ian Allan Publishing Ltd., 2016), p.57; p.59.

89. Rayner, pp.277-278.

90. Hidden, p.125, paras.13.47-13.48; Recommendation 36.

91. British Railways Board, *CLAPHAM JUNCTION RAILWAY ACCIDENT: The Implementation of the Recommendations of Sir Anthony Hidden QC* (19 February 1990), p.10. (Hereafter, '*Clapham Implementation 1*'.)
92. British Railways Board, *CLAPHAM JUNCTION RAILWAY ACCIDENT: The Implementation of the Recommendations of Sir Anthony Hidden QC, Third Progress Report* (21 February 1991), p.6. (Hereafter, '*Clapham Implementation 3*'.); *Clapham Implementation 1*, p.5. Hidden Recommendation 18. (BR's criteria became known as 'Hidden 18' as a result of the recommendation).
93. *Clapham Implementation 3*, p.6.
94. BRB Clapham, p.25, para.6.6.8.
95. *Clapham Implementation 3*, p.7, in response to Hidden Recommendation 20.
96. *Clapham Implementation 1*, pp.4–5.
97. Both are referred to in *Clapham Implementation 3*, p.5.
98. See Clive Kessell, 'Clapham 25 Years On: A Personal Analysis', *IRSE News*, No.196 (January 2014), pp.2–8 (pp.4–5).
99. *Clapham Implementation 1*, p.1, in response to Hidden Recommendation 1.
100. *Clapham Implementation 3*, p.3, in response to BR's own recommendation: 'Review the testing procedures for S&T work, clearly showing those tests which must be done prior to commissioning the work […]'. BRB Clapham, p.25, para.6.6.9; and in response to Hidden Recommendation 9.
101. *Clapham Implementation 3*, p.5.
102. BR Board, *Safety Plan 1991* (London: BRB, 1991), p.23; British Railways Board, *Safety Plan 1992* (London: BRB, 1992), p.13.
103. *Clapham Implementation 3*, p.4.
104. *Clapham Implementation 1*, p.13.
105. *Clapham Implementation 1*, p.13 (in response to Hidden Recommendation 40).
106. *Clapham Implementation 3*, p.14 (and ibid).
107. *Railway Safety: Report on the safety record of the railways in Great Britain during 1988* (London: HMSO, 1989), p.5 (and ibid).

108. Hidden, p.194, para.16; p.143, paras.15.33-15.34. Department of Transport, *Purley*, p.3, paras.1.11-1.13; Department of Transport, *Bellgrove*, p.2, para.7.

109. Ministry of Transport, *Harrow & Wealdstone*, p.24, para.84 (and ibid).

110. Ibid, para. 86.

111. BRB Clapham, p.23, para.4.11.3.

112. Department of Transport, *Colwich*, p. 1.

113. Cited in Gourvish 2, p.356 (and ibid).

114. *Clapham Implementation 1*, p.14.

115. Staff, 'Sir Robert…the end of an era', *Rail* (April 5-18 1990) p.5 (and ibid); Gourvish 2, p.138. Re Plasser, see Gourvish 2, p.213.

116. It had also become 'strategic'. See Health and Safety Technology and Management Ltd., *Strategic Safety Management: A Three Day Training Course Workbook Prepared for British Railways Board*, v2.01 (London: Health and Safety Technology and Management Ltd., May 1991).

117. Gourvish 2, p.138; The first Reid's final salary was £90,950, the second Reid's starting salary some £200,000. Ibid, p.559, note 180.

118. Gourvish 2, p.344.

119. BRB, *Safety Plan 1991*, p.3 (and ibid).

120. Richard Clarke, 'The Shadow Franchise 1988-1991: The First Steps to Privatisation – Winning Hearts and Minds', *Backtrack*, November 2021, pp.623-629 (p.627).

121. Editorial, 'The Quality business', *Modern Railways*, August 1990, p.393; Ford was describing the Anglo–Danish conference on quality in January 1989. Roger Ford, 'British Rail Pursues a Quality Culture', *Modern Railways*, August 1990, pp.401-404 (p.401) (and ibid).

122. *Clapham Implementation 3*, p.9.

123. Quoted in Ford, *Modern Railways*, August 1990, p.402.

124. Rayner, p.8.

125. Burrage made this comment when Sir Robert Reid visited the S&T Management in February 1990. Quoted in Gourvish 2, p.378 (and ibid).

126. *Clapham Implementation 3*, p.15; Gourvish 2, p.354 (and ibid). Regional Railways covered BR's secondary routes, such as those in East Anglia and

across the Pennines, plus the local commuter networks in conurbations other than London.

127. Gourvish 2, p.354 (and ibid).

128. HM Railway Inspectorate, *RAILWAY ACCIDENT AT COWDEN: A report of the inquiry into the collision between two passenger trains which occurred at Cowden on 15 October 1994* (London: HMSO, 1996), p.31, para.143; p.7, para.25.

129. Health and Safety Executive, *A report of the collision that occurred on 8 January 1991 at Cannon Street Station* (London: HMSO, 1992), p.v.

130. Health and Safety Executive, *Cannon Street*, pp.35-36, para.247.

131. Ibid, p.38, paras.270-271.

132. HM Railway Inspectorate, *Cowden*, p.39; Gourvish 2, p. 355.

133. British Railways Board, *Automatic Train Protection* (London: BRB, 1994), p.8.

134. Ibid.

135. Staff, 'Sir Bob calls for more investment', *Rail* (March 6-19 1991), p.7.

136. Murray Brown, 'THE *RAIL* INTERVIEW with: Malcolm Rifkind, Secretary of State for Transport', *Rail* (May 15-28, 1991), pp.30-31, p.31; Gourvish 2, p.266.

137. Hidden, p.139, para. 15.12; the Rt Hon Lord Cullen PC and Professor John Uff, QC FREng, *The Joint Inquiry into Train Protection Systems* (London: Health & Safety Commission, 2001), p.85, para.9.2 (and ibid).

138. Railways Act 1993 (available at http://www.legislation.gov.uk/ukpga/1993/43/contents/enacted; accessed 8 April 2020). The re-organisation process had begun mid-1993, before the Act became law (November).

139. At the Central Criminal Court in June 1991, BR pleaded guilty to charges under Sections 2 and 3 of the Health and Safety at Work Etc Act 1974. Gourvish 2, p.342.

140. The Law Commission, *LAW COM No. 237: Legislating the Criminal Code INVOLUNTARY MANSLAUGHTER Item 11 of the Sixth Programme of Law Reform: Criminal Law* (London: The Stationery Office, 4 March 1996). See p.5, paras. 1.14-1.15. The Act itself would be enacted in 2007.

141. Professor John Uff QC FREng, *The Southall Rail Accident Inquiry Report* (London: Health & Safety Commission, 2000), Annex 08 (transcript of Harrison's signal post telephone conversation with the signaller), p. 260.

142. Uff, pp.9-10, paras. 1.13-1.14; p.10, para.1.15.

143. Ibid, p.19, para.2.6; p.17, para.2.1.

144. The Rt Hon Lord Cullen PC, *The Ladbroke Grove Rail Inquiry, Part 1 Report* (London: Health & Safety Commission, 2001), pp.13-18, paras.3.1-3.27; p.7, para.2.1.

145. Cullen, p.58, paras.5.30-5.33 (ibid).

146. Ibid, p.60, para.5.40.

147. Ibid, pp.61-62, para.5.48 (and ibid).

148. Ibid, p.13, para.3.3.

149. Ibid, p.54, para.5.17.

150. Cited in ibid, p.68, paras.5.73-5.74.

151. Ibid, p.80, para.5.111.

152. Ibid, p.4, para.1.15; p.3, para. 1.10; p.5, para. 1.18; pp.3-4, para.1.12.

153. Ibid, p.109, p.7.25.

154. Ibid, p.58, para.5.32; p.109, p.7.25.

155. Ibid, p.129, para.7.99; p.113, para.7.41.

156. Ibid, p.259, Appendix 4, para.20.

157. Professor John Uff QC FREng, *The Southall Rail Accident Inquiry Report* (London: Health & Safety Commission, 2000), p.75, paras.6.27-6.28.

158. While TPWS will demand a brake application, note that it is not *guaranteed* to stop a train from passing a signal at danger. It can also be overridden, or reset by the driver, as the incident at Wootton Bassett Junction on 7 March 2015 would demonstrate. See Rail Accident Investigation Branch, *Signal passes at danger on approach to Wootton Bassett Junction, Wiltshire, 7 March 2015* (Derby: RAIB, 2016).

159. Uff-Cullen, *Joint Inquiry into Train Protection Systems*, p.12, para.11.25.

160. See https://www.ertms.net/deployment-world-map/ (accessed 12 February 2022).

161. This accident, which occurred at Great Heck on the East Coast Main Line, also involved a secondary collision with a freight train.

162. Office of Rail Regulation, *Train Derailment at Hatfield: A Final Report by the Independent Investigation Board* (London: ORR, July 2006), p.7, para.1.2; p.20, para.2.4.

163. Ibid, pp.25–26, paras.2.18–2.22; p.1.

164. Ibid, p.10, para.1.18; p.12, para.1.21.

165. Ibid, p.16, para.1.37.

166. Railway Safety, *Formal Inquiry – Final Report: Derailment of Passenger Train 1D38 1210 King's Cross to Leeds between Welham Green and Hatfield on 17 October 2000* (London: Railway Safety, 2001, pp.47–49, para.6.4.2; ORR Hatfield, p.17, para.1.38.

167. Railway Safety Hatfield, p.129, para.13.2.1.

168. ORR Hatfield, p.53, para.5.6.

169. Railway Safety Hatfield, p.51, para.6.5.4.

170. ORR Hatfield, p.17, para.1.38 (and ibid).

171. Ibid, p.17, para.1.39.

172. Railway Safety Hatfield, p.57, para.6.7.1.

173. ORR Hatfield, p.121, para.8.97.

174. Ibid, p.95 (table).

175. Ibid, p.91, paras.7.53–7.54.

176. Ibid, p.116, para.8.69.

177. Ibid, p.118, para.8.77; ibid. Para.8.78.

178. Ibid, p.119, para.8.81; ibid, para.8.84.

179. Railway Safety Hatfield, p.53, para.6.6.3.1.

180. ORR Hatfield, p.64, para.5.40 (point 8).

181. Railway Safety Hatfield, p.52, para.6.6.2.

182. ORR Hatfield, p.86, paras.7.32–7.33.

183. Ibid, p.88, para.7.37 (and ibid).

184. Ibid, p.99, para.7.86 (and ibid).

185. Ibid, p.114, para.8.57 (and ibid).

186. Roger Ford, 'Informed Sources: Williams-Shapps Plan – who will run the railway?', *Modern Railways*, July 2021, pp.36–38, p.37.

187. ORR Hatfield, p.107, para. 8.25.

188. Ibid, p.108, paras.8.27–8.29.

189. HSE, *Railway Safety Statistics Bulletin 1998-99*, cited in Wolmar, p.168.

190. Gourvish 3, p.67.
191. Christian Wolmar, *On the Wrong Line: How Ideology and Incompetence Wrecked Britain's Railways* (London: Aurum Press Ltd, 2005), p.254.
192. ORR, Hatfield, p.109, para. 8.32.
193. Cited in Gourvish 3, p.79.
194. See also Gourvish 3, p.67; p.72.
195. Correspondence with Professor Anson Jack 1 August 2020. See also Gourvish 3, p.77 (re West Coast Main Line).
196. See Gourvish 3, p.130; pp.179–189.
197. HSE, *Train Derailment at Potters Bar 10 May 2002* (London: HMSO, 2003), pp.i–ii, para.5., p.26, paras. 3.4–3.7.
198. Ibid, para.3.5.
199. Ibid, pp.i–ii, para.5.Ibid, p.iv, para.10.
200. The Rt Hon Lord Cullen PC, *The Ladbroke Grove Rail Inquiry, Part 2 Report* (London: Health & Safety Commission, 2001), p.175; p.177.
201. Recommendation 57 ('The responsibility of the HSE for the investigation of rail accidents should be transferred to an independent body, here referred to for convenience as the RAIB'). Ibid, p.177. The Branch became fully operational in October 2005.
202. Rail Accident Investigation Branch, *Derailment at Grayrigg, 23 February 2007*, Version 5 (Derby: RAIB, 2011), p.127, para.516.
203. Ibid, p.128, para. 519.
204. Rail Accident Investigation Branch, *Serious irregularity at Cardiff East Junction, 29 December 2016* (Derby: RAIB, 2017), p.29 (and ibid).
205. The press release in which these statements were made is part of the webpage for the investigation report. See https://www.gov.uk/government/news/report-152017-serious-irregularity-at-cardiff-east-junction (accessed 7 September 2019) (and ibid).
206. Rail Accident Investigation Branch, *Collision at Waterloo, 15 August 2017* (Derby: RAIB, 2018), p.51.
207. Ibid, p.47 (and ibid).
208. Hidden, p.163, paras.17.1–17.2 (cited in RAIB Waterloo, p.47, para.190).
209. Roger Ford, 'George report emphasises local expertise', *Modern Railways* (April 2019), pp.32–35 (p.33).

210. Andrew Haines, 'Restoring pride in operations', *Modern Railways* (March 2019), pp.6-9 (p.7) and ibid.

211. Ibid, p.8.

212. Rayner, pp.211-12.

213. *Clapham Junction Inquiry: Recommendations Submitted on Behalf of Clifford Hale Esq*, p.3, Recommendation 3.4. London TravelWatch archive file 611437728.

214. For ERTMS on the Cambrian, see Rail Accident Investigation Branch, *Loss of safety critical signalling data on the Cambrian Coast line, 20 October 2017* (Derby: RAIB, 2019).

215. Roger Ford, 'Informed Sources: Yaw damper problems hit CAF and Hitachi', *Modern Railways*, June 2021, pp.28-32; p.32.

216. Marcus Dacre, 'Effective systems? Working for National Air Traffic Services during 9/11', *Rail Safety Review 56* (London: RSSB, September 2021), pp.1-2.

217. Carl Macrae, *Close Calls: Managing Risk and Resilience in Airline Flight Safety* (Palgrave Macmillan: 2014), p.122.

218. Sir John Elliot, *On and Off the Rails* (London: George Allen & Unwin Ltd., 1982), pp.118-119.

219. Baker Panel, *The Report of the BP Refineries Independent Safety Review Panel* (BP, 2007), p. i.

220. Department of Transport, *Lockington*, p. 1, paras.1-2.

221. Professor P. F. Stott CBE FEng, *Automatic Open Crossings: A Review of Safety* (London: Department of Transport, 1987), pp.13-14, paras.15.10-15.14.

222. Department of Transport, *Glanrhyd*, p.25, para.206

223. BR's Director of Civil Engineering produced an Action Plan to identify bridges susceptible to damage by river action. BR also issued a handbook entitled *Assessment of the Risk of Scour* in May 1989. Ibid, p.26, para.281; https://www.gov.uk/government/news/report-222016-structural-failure-at-lamington-viaduct.

224. Rail Accident Investigation Unit, *Malahide Viaduct Collapse on the Dublin to Belfast Line, on the 21st August 2009* (Blackrock: RAIU, 2010), para. 5.2-5.3, p.14; p.iv; p.v.

225. European Commission, *Memorandum on Lifelong Learning* (Brussels: The European Commission, 2000), p. 3.

226. Annie Brooking, *Corporate Memory: Strategies for knowledge management* (Andover: Cengage Learning EMEA, 1999), p. 2.

227. See JR East, *Accident History Exhibition Hall* (Tokyo: JR East, 2008) and JR East Group, *Sustainability Report 2019* (Tokyo: JR East, 2020), pp.10-11 (and ibid).

228. RAIB, *Waterloo*, p.52, para.196 (and ibid).

229. Long, Roger and Greg Morse, *Learning from History: Lessons from past accidents 1981-2017* (produced by *Rail* magazine, 2017). The document may be downloaded free of charge via: https://www.railmagazine.com/special-reports/network-rail
The Ladbroke Grove presentation was written and presented by the author, with slides by his RSSB colleague Wayne Murphy.

230. The RAIB film may be found via this page of its website: https://www.gov.uk/government/news/report-182017-overturning-of-a-tram-at-sandilands-junction-croydon RED 49, in which the author makes some sort of appearance, is free to RSSB member companies via the RSSB website: https://www.rssb.co.uk/safety-and-health/learning-from-experience/red-programmes/red-49-past-at-danger.

231. For Safety Central, see https://safety.networkrail.co.uk/.9

232. JR East Group, *Sustainability Report 2019* (Tokyo: JR East, 2020), p.35.

233. James Reason, *Managing the Risks of Organisational Accidents* (Aldershot: Ashgate Publishing Ltd., 1997), p.108.

234. Rayner, p.212.

235. Ibid, p.352.

236. Desmond Fennell OBE QC, *Investigation into the King's Cross Underground Fire* (London: HMSO, 1988), p.17, para.12.

237. Per Professor Anson Jack. Correspondence with author, 14 September 2020.

238. Rayner, p.374.

239. Ibid, p.376.

240. Rail Accident Investigation Branch, *Wrongside signalling failure and derailment at Dalwhinnie, Badenoch and Strathspey, 10 April 2021* (Derby: RAIB, 2022), p.49, para.151.

241. See Greg Morse, 'Wrongside Failure in the Scottish Highlands', *IRSE News* (February 2023), pp.26-7.

242. See Charles Haddon-Cave QC, *The Nimrod Report – an independent review into the broader issues surrounding the loss of the RAF Nimrod MR2 Aircraft XV230 in Afghanistan in 2006* (HMSO, 2009), p.491.

243. See *The Yorkshire Ripper Files: A Very British Crime Story* (BBC4, 2019), dir. Liza Williams.

244. Rail Accident Investigation Branch, *Derailment of a passenger train at Carmont, Aberdeenshire, 12 August 2020* (Derby: RAIB, 2022), p.42, para.14 (and ibid).

245. Ibid, p. 103, para.169.

246. Rail Accident Investigation Branch, *Structural failure caused by scour at Lamington Viaduct, South Lanarkshire, 31 December 2015* (Derby: RAIB, 2016), p.42, para.129.

247. Rail Accident Investigation Branch, *Derailment due to a landslip, and subsequent collision, Watford, 16 September 2016* (Derby: RAIB, 2017), p.7.

248. Roger Ford, 'Informed Sources: Williams-Shapps Plan – who will run the railway?', *Modern Railways*, July 2021, pp.36–38, p.37.

249. Clarke, p.628; Ford, 'Williams-Shapps', p.37.

250. Keith Williams, *Great British Railways: The Williams-Shapps Plan for Rail* (London: HMSO, 2021), p.34.

Index